Thank-You!

Josh Clifson

Financial Excellence

A Treasury of Wisdom and Inspiration

by
John Avanzini

Harrison House
Tulsa, Oklahoma

Unless otherwise specified, all Scripture quotations are taken from the *King James Version* of the Bible.

Scripture verses marked TLB are taken from *The Living Bible* Copyright © 1971. Used by permission of Tyndale House Publishers, Inc., Wheaton, Illinois 60189. All rights reserved.

Financial Excellence
ISBN 0-89274-856-7
Copyright © 1991 by His Image Ministries
Box 1057
Hurst, Texas 76053

Published by Harrison House, Inc.
P. O. Box 35035
Tulsa, Oklahoma 74153

Contents

Introduction

This book represents the wisdom and God-given inspiration I have gained concerning Christian finances over the last several years.

What I have learned about God's plan for His children's financial well-being has come from more than thirty years of Bible study. In some cases God has shown me some very basic truths through special revelation of His Word.

I have seen God's desire and financial plan for us plundered — individually and for the Church as a whole. The devil — our greatest enemy — has robbed from us continually. However, I have also seen knowledge and right action triumph over the deceiver — in my life and that of many others.

Our Heavenly Father's plan for our finances is three-fold:

1) to provide His children their needs.

2) to provide for the preaching of the Gospel.

3) to provide plenty for His children so that they can give joyfully to others.

This book is written to accomplish two purposes:

1) to help those who need an immediate turn-around in their personal finances, to be blessed of God so they can be a blessing to others.

2) to assist those who are already enjoying the Lord's financial blessings to be an even greater blessing to others.

This book is divided into three parts, combining needed general information with very practical, step-by-step instruction.

Part I gives an overview of God's desire and plan for your financial abundance, as well as information about just how the thief will try to rob you — to rip you off — often before that abundance even reaches your hands! You need to know your enemy to effectively fight him!

Part II outlines God's plan, requirements and laws for reaping the financial harvest you need or want. You will see how tithes and offerings are essential to obeying the laws of the harvest.

Part III speaks of debt — about how and why we enter into it, the special responsibility it holds for Christians and, most importantly, specific suggestions as to how we can reduce and eliminate it while we wait to reap the full harvests God has promised us.

It is my sincere prayer that this book will be a blessing to you, that you will use the knowledge in it to help others prosper and be blessed.

Part I
God, Your Finances and the Thief

1
God Wants Abundance for Us

C hild of God, I alert you to the fact that Satan is clearly waging a battle of containment against the saints of God.

He is not nearly as concerned with driving you backwards as he is with *containing* you where you are, and keeping you from getting where God wants you to go.

Can you identify with that?

In your prayer life, if you desire a greater walk with God, you will find that the devil will let you continue to pray at your current prayer level. But as soon as you try to break into a new dimension of prayer, frequent distractions occur.

People come to visit you. Your hours will change at work. The phone will ring. Any time you start to move decisively forward, Satan increases the *battle of containment.*

You may have experienced this battle of containment in the realm of holiness or sanctification. You achieve a certain walk, then all of a sudden, you stop growing. You do not especially go backwards, but you just find it increasingly difficult to move forward.

Please understand *that* is the stark reality of Satan's battle of containment against you!

As you start to grow in the revelations I am bringing to you in this book, you will quickly realize that at this very moment the devil is waging a powerful battle of containment in your finances.

He will tell you that *you are getting along okay, so just don't rock the boat!*

He will even try to deceive you into thinking that this book is *just another prosperity message, but do not be distracted!*

Please recognize that this is the *vital Biblical message* that your spirit man has been hungering after — the message of deliverance from the ever-present insufficiency!

Do not let the devil continue to contain you in your present financial dilemma!

One of the primary deceptions that so many Christians believe is that the Bible says, "*the truth will set you free.*"

The Bible does not say that the truth will set you free. What the Bible says is something very different. Read carefully now what it actually says:

And ye shall *know* the truth, and the truth shall make you free.

John 8:32

Do you see it? It is *the truth you know* that has the divine power to set you free. Please hear me. The only truth that can set you free is the truth *that you personally know.* You can walk around with the truth (the Bible) in your right hand, placed lovingly over your breast; you can walk around with that precious Bible right over your lungs, and still have a horrible cancer grow in those lungs that will eventually snuff out your very life.

Many Christians die prematurely in the presence of truth, with the Bible on the nightstand next to their death bed. But keep this in mind. The *presence* of truth cannot and does not heal! You see, it is not the presence of truth, but *the knowledge* of truth that has power and sets you free. Hear the Scriptures well:

And ye shall *know* the truth, and the truth shall make you free.

John 8:32

It is time to order our lives line upon line, precept upon precept, concept upon Biblical concept. We must build a foundation of truth so powerful that Satan cannot contain it.

Now hear me well. I want you to break out of the containment building that Satan has constructed around your finances.

Please, be very careful, and do not mistake *a mere penetration* of Satan's containment in your finances *as a breakthrough.* There is a vast difference between a penetration and a breakthrough, and I want nothing less for you from this book than a *total breakthrough!*

Perhaps you have made an occasional penetration in the wall of containment Satan has placed around your finances. Maybe you have already gained enough bits and pieces of knowledge to understand that God does not intend for you to be poor, and that He has a Biblical plan of abundance for your life.

I want you to go beyond bits and pieces. It is time for you to start gathering *great quantities* of spiritual power. When this power is complete, it will bring about a *total breakthrough* in your finances which will move you permanently beyond Satan's containment!

Remember, any time you want to break through a spiritual barrier, *it takes great spiritual energy*; it takes the power of God working through you!

Without a doubt, it is the most potent type of power in the universe. As you understand the *truth* of this powerful revelation, as you *know* this truth by putting it into *practical application* in your life, you will experience a powerful new day in your finances, a true and lasting spiritual breakthrough.

Surely you have experienced the *difference* between penetration and breakthrough in your own life.

Remember when you first heard about sanctification? As you began to gather bits and pieces of Biblical truth on this subject, your spiritual energy level rose until finally you had enough spiritual power for a penetration. How wonderful the land of sanctification looked beyond Satan's wall of containment. Remember how you peered through the hole in that wall and said, "Look how wonderfully sanctified my life could be if I could only break through this wall of containment?"

The breakthrough only came when you allowed that energy, that input of Biblical truth, to continue and continue to grow. It took effort. It literally took a violent effort, not casual daydreaming and wishing, to accomplish it.

The same energy that brought you your previous breakthrough, the same level of effort that swept you to past victories, must now come forth for you to achieve a financial breakthrough as you are guided by this book. You must *gather* many Biblical principles relating to the financing of God's end-time harvest, and then *apply* these principles today and tomorrow. Not so you can make just a little hole and peer through a small, rapidly closing penetration, but so you can achieve nothing less than a *total breakthrough*!

Satan has contained you in your finances long enough! Jericho's walls must come down!

If there is still any doubt that Satan is containing you in your finances, let me quickly prove to you that he is.

Right now, you can think of several people who are not as smart nor as qualified as you are who are making more money than you make. How can this be unless the devil has put an invisible wall around your financial potential? You see, the devil does not care how much money non-Christians make, because as long as they control it, their money will not be used to finance the preaching of the Gospel to those who have not yet heard the message of Jesus Christ.

The rock stars will never finance the gospel. The raunchy movie producers will not give one dime for the next major evangelistic crusade.

That's why the devil does not contain them like he does you and me! You see, financing the end-time harvest is up to you and me as born-again Christians. If you do not have the financial breakthrough God wants you to have, His Church will never rise to the full level of the vision that God has for it.

That's why Satan wants to contain you in your current financial strata. You know I am telling the truth. If you make $200 extra one month, he sees to it that the tire will blow out on your car, or the water heater will go out at your home.

Don't you see, it is the devil who wages this continual battle of containment against your finances?

Every time you try to enter into a financial breakthrough, he will come against you, and the only way to smash and destroy the wall of containment around your finances is through a violent, highly energetic act on your part.

I don't use the word "violent" at my choosing, but God's Word tells us to literally get violent and use our God-given force (spiritual energy).

And from the days of John the Baptist until now the kingdom of heaven suffereth violence, and *the violent take it by force.*

Matthew 11:12

If you want to make a breakthrough in your finances, then determine right now in your mind that you are going to take *whatever action is necessary* to crush the devil's wall of containment around your finances, removing the limitations of that invisible wall and breaking through, by force and violence, into a new level of understanding *and* knowledge in the area of your finances.

You probably already have much spiritual energy from God's Word in you. This book will put even more and more of that spiritual energy into you through a better and broader understanding of His Word.

All of a sudden, you will realize that His Word is concentrated so strongly in you that you now have enough spiritual energy to come with *violent spiritual force* against the invisible wall that is resisting you and pushing against your finances, and blow those walls asunder!

You will charge forth into newly discovered wealth and prosperity, *receiving literally more than enough* to help finance every worthwhile Christian ministry that God directs you to help.

I think that you can now see that if you really want this financial breakthrough, it will take more than a penetration. Most of the teaching on finances today only takes you to a point of penetration. Although you have hungered for this breakthrough, you probably never have possessed enough of the spiritual power, the concentrated energy, to break forth and walk out of those satanic walls of containment, into true Biblical financial success and freedom.

Child of God, you are at a critical point!

Now is the time for *your* breakthrough! Read. Study. Absorb. Then take *violent action!*

Begin to seize the financial power that you have according to the Word of God!

Get Violent in God

"Why is violent action necessary?" you might ask.

You see, those old teachings, those old traditions have made the Word of God and your Heavenly Father's desire for you to abound ineffective. Deuteronomy 8:18a is a good example:

> **But thou shalt remember the Lord thy God: for it is he that giveth thee *power to get wealth*. . . .**

When was the last time you heard anyone give a sermon on *that* Scripture? You see, there are walls around those Scriptures containing the Body of Christ's financial advancement and expansion.

Many of you were brought up in a day when poverty was erroneously deemed by well-meaning preachers and teachers to be glorious and Godly! Unfortunately, the "poverty is holy" doctrine still hangs around in the back of your mind today. Many of you *still believe* there is something wrong with a man who has a lot of money.

I used to think, "Oh God, if I just had enough. Lord, just give me enough to provide for my wife, Pat, and our kids."

Have you ever prayed a prayer like that? Sure you have, but don't ever pray it again!

As this book progresses, I will show you that it is impossible for you to be *the Christian God intends for you to be* with "just enough."

Think about the day you got saved. Your salvation was absolutely free. It did not cost you one penny to get saved. I remember walking into the First Baptist Church of Largo, Florida. They treated me like a king. There was not a charge for anything. My salvation did not cost me one cent.

But when I came back saved the next Wednesday night, and from that day on, I have been handing out money everywhere I go!

Child of God, do you understand what I am talking about here? It costs money to bring in God's harvest, and the Church of our Lord and Savior will never have enough to do it as long as saints have *"just enough."* We can only bring in the end-time harvest if God's saints learn how to have *more than enough* to supply the funds needed to do the great work that God has put before us.

Let's begin generating some spiritual energy in the area of your finances. Let's begin right now by destroying one old concept that must go from your mind before you can move any further in your finances.

Let's establish this new thought in your mind:

There is nothing wrong with me and my family living the good life!

It is God's portion for me.

Behold that which I have seen: it is good and comely for one to eat and to drink, and *to enjoy the good of all of his labour* that he taketh under

the sun all the days of his life, which God giveth him: *for it is his portion.*

Every man also to whom God hath given *riches* and *wealth*, and hath given him power to eat thereof, and *to take his portion*, and to rejoice in his labour; *this is the gift of God.*

Ecclesiastes 5:18,19

The good life is your portion!

Most Christians get it in their minds that there is great insufficiency in the world, and that we must live all of our lives in that insufficiency.

Let me assure you, that is not God's way. He says, "There is more than enough." He says, "The good life is your portion!"

Do you see how Satan is waging a battle in your mind, a battle of containment? It is hard for many to grasp just "having enough," let alone grasping that God intends for you to have *more than enough.*

Remember, it is the world's method to have its population operate in insufficiency, shortage, and want. They feel that's the way to keep prices up — through contrived, manipulated shortage!

But do not forget, we are not of this world, and our God and King declares that the basis of His Kingdom is *abundance!* He plainly says:

. . . I am come that they might have life, and that they might have it *more abundantly.*

John 10:10b

You see, the lifestyle God has chosen for us *is* His abundance. This abundant lifestyle is the type of a breakthrough that you are heading for if you do not let the devil contain you in your current strata of income — through distraction, ringing phones, and other devices — to get you away from *knowing* the truth of God's Word that I am trying to teach you.

Oh, saint of God, press on, and you will stomp on the devil. God says the devil will soon be bruised under your feet:

And the God of peace shall bruise Satan under your feet shortly.

Romans 16:20a

Notice the last portion of Ecclesiastes 5:19 says that the good life is your portion, it is "the gift of God," and you have the power to eat your portion.

I can just hear some of you saying, "Well, Brother John, if wealth and the good life are God's gifts to me, then why don't I have them?"

If you know anything about God, you know that God does not hand out all of His gifts on a silver platter. A good illustration of God's nature is seen when He "gave" the promised land to Israel. It was a gift, but they had to *violently fight* to receive it. There was not one square foot that came easily, yet Scripture clearly states it was God's gift to them. God has set aside a portion of the world's wealth for you. It is yours for the taking. But to take control of that wealth involves your decision to *violently fight* and take it out of the control of God's enemies, just as Israel took the promised land from the enemies of God (Please notice that this fight is in the spirit world. I am not advocating an armed conflict).

Notice through this personal illustration how important it is to know the truth if you expect to be set free by that truth.

In my early ministry, I was Dr. John Avanzini, pastor of a fundamental denominational church. I was so narrow-minded in my view of Scripture and my denomination being right about every single doctrine that I could look through a keyhole with both eyes!

In those early ministry years, when I walked into a hospital, it was like the hospital was having a visit from the angel of death. I would place my hands on a man with a common cold and it would quickly turn into double pneumonia. When I went into the cardiac ward, the Intensive Care nurses would panic.

"Here comes Dr. Avanzini," they would cry. Then, those heart machines that normally go "beep, beep, beep" would start going crazy, and just go "beeeeeeeeeeeeep."

I did not *know* that the stripes Jesus received on my behalf and on the behalf of the world had given me *power* to lay hands on the sick and that they would have to recover.

You see, you cannot walk in a truth you do not *know.* Oh, I bought my study books in a bookstore where people knew that truth. I personally was around the truth every day. I earned a doctorate at the Baptist Theological Seminary in Shreveport, Louisiana. But I didn't *know* about the fullness of the Holy Ghost.

You cannot have the full benefit of a truth unless you *know* it. Finally, one day I had a breakthrough. I discovered that the Bible says, *and means,* that I could, right now in the twentieth century, lay hands on the sick and they would recover!

. . . They shall lay hands on the sick, and they shall recover.

Mark 16:18b

Pain just left people when I prayed for them. Symptoms vanished. Terminal cases were healed with a touch — one such case with just a word from the pulpit to a man diagnosed terminal.

I experienced the difference between head knowledge and heart knowledge, the difference between *logos* and *rhema*. Logos is the written Word, but *rhema* is the Word of God *living* in you!

Suddenly, a whole new flow began for me! Wisdom came to me. Healing functioned through me. Once I really *knew* the truth, then I could operate in it.

Right now, you may be powerless in the area of your finances. You may be the victim of your environment which taught you that "poverty is Godly," and which has brought about a poverty atmosphere around you.

Begin now to chisel at those old, false concepts. Start this minute to begin receiving more of your financial breakthrough by absorbing the *rhema* of this incredible Scripture:

But thou shalt remember the Lord thy God: for it is he that giveth thee [that means you] **power to get wealth. . . .**

Deuteronomy 8:18a

Read that Scripture out loud several times right now. You have very possibly never read anything like it before. It goes against so much of what you have been taught. But there it is in your Bible, staring at you. Your breakthrough cannot come unless you cooperate by *violently* pressing against the restraints of Satan that make you question the validity of this Word from God. Read it again and again.

God Himself has given *you* the *power to get wealth!* Isn't that amazing?

You have the power to get wealth, and that power has been given to you by God. Say it out loud: "I have been given the power to get wealth by the God of heaven."

Say it ten times. Say it with confidence. Listen to yourself saying it. If God says this about you, then you can say it about yourself. For the rest of your life, say this to yourself several times each day: *"God has given me the power to get wealth."*

First, receive the *logos* of this statement, the written word; it *is* written in your Holy Bible.

Next, receive the *rhema* of this statement by beginning to *operate* that word in your life.

To *operate* the *rhema* of this statement, you must understand the total context of the verse. *This is very important. Do not miss a word.*

This revelation is more than the "Cadillac Faith" prosperity being taught in so many messages on finances. Although that message is based in a partial truth — it does not go far enough. God does not mind the saints driving Cadillacs, Lincolns, or Hondas. But if that's all the message you hear, then you've totally missed God!

You have thrown away *the pearl* and kept the oyster shell. Let me tell you a story about such a situation.

There was a man who had been listening to the tapes of a certain prosperity preacher, and he was all excited about God making him rich — real quick.

One day he drove up to the church in a big, beautiful new luxury car, and parked it right in the front of the building in the most conspicuous parking space. The preacher, seeing him pull up, asked him, "Where did you get such a nice car?" to which the man replied, "Preacher, God gave me that car."

The preacher congratulated the man, and agreed with him, saying, "That looks like the kind of car God would give."

As they both walked all around the car, the preacher noticed the man's special, personalized license plate. It read, "PRAYED 4."

For the next ten to twelve months, everything seemed just great. Every Sunday, this seemingly prosperous fellow would drive up to the church in his big, beautiful luxury car that was now affectionately being called "Old PRAYED 4." His seeming success caused everyone to feel very envious, and even somewhat convicted that their faith for wealth was not at this man's level.

But one Sunday, here came this same man, not in his luxury car, but this time in, of all things, an old Nash automobile. You remember how they looked. They resembled an upside-down bathtub with the windshield in the blunt end. Well, he slowly drove up in this old car and parked way in the back of the church parking lot in the most obscure parking space.

The preacher, seeing this obvious deviation from what had become his normal entrance, went over to this fellow, and asked, "Hey, where's 'Old PRAYED 4'?"

He said, "Pastor, they repossessed it, and everything else I own is in bankruptcy."

Can you imagine, they repossessed the car God had supposedly given him! Here we see the all too common end to the "get riches for your own benefit" gospel: disappointment and loss of credibility and our own loss of witness for Christ.

The preacher of our story then put his arms around this fellow and lovingly told him, "Brother, listen to me carefully. I thank God for the teachers we have in our land. But man, you are obviously missing it. Come on into God's house today and start hearing what God really says about your finances, and how they relate to *His purposes,* and not how they relate to *your* purposes. Start learning the prosperity message in the proper context.

"If your motive for giving is right with God, and if you really *know* God's intentions for the prosperity you receive from Him, *then* if you still desire a nice car, God will give it to you. God does not mind you having a nice car, if that is what you really want. And this time, when He gives it to you, it will be better than your last car, and you won't have to have some goofy license plate like 'PRAYED 4' on it. With the car that God gives, you can have a *real* license plate, one that says 'PAID 4.' "

Friend please, begin to hear me on this. Deuteronomy 8:18 tells you that God has given you the *power* to get wealth. But read the verse *in context* and you will see *why* God is giving you that power!

. . . that he may establish his covenant which he sware unto thy fathers, as it is this day.
Deuteronomy 8:18b

God has given you power to get wealth so that His covenant can be established. The word "established" here means "founded and grounded" financially so that no economic problems could ever uproot or overthrow the orderly operation of that covenant on the earth.

Do you really think that God wants the state of the national or local economy to affect the operation of His Church and His chosen ministries?

Do you really think that God would want every economic slump in the natural realm to disrupt the ministry of His Church? *Of course not!*

Do you understand? God has a plan for His Church (the saints) to be so established in finances that literally no problem in the economy will affect the church's economy: Good times, bad times, depression, recession, it makes no difference. God intends for His Church to grow and flourish no matter what the world might be facing in its godless economics.

God has given every one of His children the *power* to get wealth so that they can be established financially to generously fund every need that arises for the operation of the covenant He made with Abraham.

That alone is the primary reason why the saints have been given the power to get wealth!

If you are seeking *first* the Kingdom of God and His righteousness, if you are using your God-given power to get wealth to establish God's Kingdom first, *then* the secondary portion of the covenant comes into play, which is adding all of these other things (your needs and wants) unto you.

> **But seek ye first the kingdom of God, and his righteousness; and *all these things* shall be added unto you.**
>
> **Matthew 6:33**

Notice *God* adds "all these things." When you effectively do *your part* of first *establishing His kingdom,* then God will do *His part* — and give you "all these things" you need and want for the good life *in abundance!*

And, you may be surprised to learn that God has a pattern of giving the wealth (or "all these things") of the wicked to His children.

As you add to your storehouse of knowledge concerning God's standard operating procedures, you will begin to discover that it is an ongoing, established, standard practice throughout history for God to fulfill the second part of Proverbs 13:22b, and transfer the wealth of the wicked to His children at the critical time of their need:

> **. . . and the wealth of the sinner** [wicked] **is laid up for the just.**
>
> **Proverbs 13:22b**

You know, I can hear you saying, "Brother John, I believe you. I believe you because I believe the Word of God. It says that the wealth of the wicked is laid up for the just, so it must be true. But being a human, my logical mind says this is all just too fantastic to be fulfilled. I have to confess that it is beyond my realm of experience. Yes, I believe the Bible, but I must be totally honest. I have never heard of the wealth being turned over in wholesale fashion to the righteous. I see from my experience that lost wicked men simply do not give away their wealth."

Please be at ease. You *have heard of this happening* time and time again. Let me now bring some of these times back to your remembrance.

How about Abram and the Egyptians? Do you remember that account in the twelfth chapter of Genesis? Abram received great wealth from the wicked Egyptians.

Keep in mind that Abram was flat broke when he arrived in Egypt. Although it can be argued that he came from rich ancestors, when he and Sarai arrived in Egypt, he definitely was not rich. He couldn't even afford to hire a bodyguard. So, upon entering Egypt, he told his wife, Sarai, to tell everyone she met that she was his sister.

Well, you know the story. Pharaoh fell in love with Sarai, and stated that he would marry her on a certain date. The Scriptures say:

> **And he** [the Pharaoh] **entreated Abram well for her sake: and he had sheep, and oxen, and he asses, and menservants, and maidservants, and she asses, and camels.**
>
> **Genesis 12:16**

This was all well and good until the Pharaoh discovered Sarai was really Abram's wife. The Pharaoh became so angry that he threw Abram out of Egypt. Note a very interesting point — Pharaoh let Abram keep all of the wealth he had given him!

> **And Pharaoh commanded his men concerning him: and they sent him away, and his wife, and *all that he had*.**
>
> **Genesis 12:20**

Notice that in one short visit to Egypt, the wealth of the wicked was quickly transferred to the just man — Abram. Notice how much wealth Abram acquired in this short time. Chapter 13, verse 2, tells us that upon Abram's departure from Egypt he had great substance:

> **And Abram was *very rich* in *cattle*, in *silver*, and in *gold*.**
>
> **Genesis 13:2**

God sent Abram, who just a short time before entered Egypt poor, out of Egypt with an abundance of cattle, silver and gold! Abram was actually *given* the wealth of wicked Egypt.

Further along in this passage, we see that Abram and Lot had acquired *so many possessions* while in Egypt that. . .**the land was not able to bear them.** (Gen. 13:6.)

They actually had such great substance that they could not dwell close together, for they needed large amounts of land to contain and sustain their great herds.

A close examination of Scripture seems to show that Lot's wealth came from his association with Abram. It is important to notice here that Abram's wealth was so excessive that even his nephew was able to prosper from his vast abundance. Clearly, this shows that when God distributes the wealth,

He doesn't mind if His children have more than enough.

Notice, however, that Lot was unable to grasp that the wealth he had been receiving was from God's hands to him. He associated his wealth with the world's economic principles working in his life. Yet, in Genesis 13:14,15 God tells Abram:

> **. . . Lift up now thine eyes, and look from the place where thou art northward, and southward, and eastward, and westward:**
>
> **For all the land which thou seest, to thee will I give it, and to thy seed for ever.**
>
> **Genesis 13:14,15**

These are not the promises of a God who wants His children to dwell in poverty, starvation and ignorance! No indeed! The God of Abram *is the God of abundance!* In verse 17, God tells Abram:

> **Arise, walk through the land in the length of it and in the breadth of it; for I will give it unto thee.**
>
> **Genesis 13:17**

That is not a God who wants His people to barely make it! He gave Abram *more than enough!*

As you study God's Word carefully, you will find that God's clearly stated intention is to take very good care of His children, especially those who walk in His footsteps and obey His will.

Also, keep in mind that God gave all of this land to Abram and his seed (the righteous). Remember that every bit of this property was once owned by wicked heathen men, and God took that land of the wicked and gave it to the just. Isn't that what we are finding more and more in our study? The wealth of the wicked is laid up for the just.

Let us now look at another case where the wealth of the wicked was transferred to the just.

Let us observe this process as it operated in the life of Isaac. He, too, experienced the God-ordained transfer of the wealth of the wicked into his possession.

While Isaac was living in his homeland, Genesis 26 tells us that he ran out of supplies because of a harsh famine, so he decided to do as his father before him had done, and go down into Egypt.

Isaac got as far as the land of the Philistines, when God told him to stop.

God told Isaac to stay out of Egypt, and to continue dwelling in the land of the wicked Philistines, a land that the famine had rendered barren and seemingly non-productive.

But God promised Isaac that if he followed His instructions (instructions you and I would probably label as "foolish"), he would prosper.

> **Sojourn in this land, and I will be with thee, and will bless thee; for unto thee, and unto thy seed, I will give all these countries, and I will perform the oath which I swore unto Abraham thy father.**
>
> **Genesis 26:3**

Some will read this passage and immediately assume that God meant an abundance of *spiritual blessings.* Oh, how we love to give our own definition to God's Word. In verse 12 of this passage, we see what God means by "blessings" in the midst of a famine.

Then Isaac sowed in that land [a land in the midst of famine], **and received in the same year an hundredfold: and the Lord blessed him.**

Genesis 26:12

In verse 14, we see a further inventory of what God had given to Isaac.

For he had possession of *flocks*, and possession of *herds*, and great *store of servants*: and *the Philistines envied him*.

Genesis 26:14

Are we to believe that the Philistines envied Isaac's spiritual heritage? Weigh that thought carefully.

Are we to believe that they envied Isaac's good standing with God? Weigh that thought carefully.

Of course not!

The Philistines envied Isaac because he had huge crops for food in the midst of famine — crops that he was able to sell for huge amounts of money to buy large flocks of sheep for meat and for clothing, and because he had a "great store" of servants to wait on his every need. In the midst of famine, Isaac cleaned out the wealth of the Philistines.

That's why the Philistines envied Isaac! He was the son of a living God who prospers His sons and daughters by giving them the wealth of the wicked.

Yes, of course, Isaac first and foremost had a deep *spiritual inheritance.* But God had also earmarked an abundant *material, earthly inheritance* for him — just as He had for Abram.

That's the same way He wants it for you now:

Every man also to whom God hath given riches and wealth, and hath given him power to

eat thereof, and to *take his portion,* and to rejoice in his labour; *this is the gift of God.*

Ecclesiastes 5:19

God gives both *spiritual and financial* wealth to His people.

Poverty is simply not a Biblical principle that applies to the obedient and industrious saints of God. It is time that Christians stop claiming that poverty is what God wants for their lives!

Friend, let's face it, *poverty is not God's perfect will for you.* To live daily on the brink of insufficiency and claim that it is God's intended status for you is a spiritual mistake. In Biblical illustration after Biblical illustration, the same truth keeps emerging:

God has a people, and God takes care of His people, in *the spiritual realm,* in *the physical realm,* and in *the financial realm.*

Hear the beloved Apostle John declare it:

Beloved, I wish above all things that thou mayest *prosper* and *be in health,* even *as thy soul prospereth.*

3 John 2

In the 31st chapter of Genesis, we *once again* see this principle of taking the wealth of the wicked and giving it to the just illustrated in the life of Jacob. If you are plagued by a crooked or unsympathetic boss who you believe hinders God's ability to flow His abundance into your life — then read this next section closely!

No one had a more crooked, stingy, unsympathetic boss than Jacob. Laban was crooked, crooked, crooked, and, he was a real tightwad! Ten times, Laban changed Jacob's compensation program! Once, Jacob worked seven years to marry Laban's beautiful daughter, only to have Laban secretly switch daughters at the wedding, and trick Jacob into a marriage with his plain daughter.

After many years of Jacob working faithfully for Laban, God instructed Jacob to "return to the land of thy fathers."

Naturally, Jacob was willing to obey.

But before he left, Jacob revealed to Laban's daughters the amazing divine principle of taking the wealth of the wicked and giving it to the just, the principle that had been operating in his life as he worked for their father Laban.

Read these verses very carefully, for they provide a major breakthrough to understanding the mind of God, and to destroying any previous conceptions you may have about what God will do for His children.

> **And ye know that with all my power I have served your father.**
>
> **And your father hath deceived me, and changed my wages ten times; *but God suffered him not to hurt me.***
>
> **If he said thus, the speckled shall be thy wages; then all the cattle bare speckled: and if he said thus, The ringstraked shall be thy hire; then bare all the cattle ringstraked.**
>
> **Thus God *hath taken away the cattle of your father, and given them to me.***
>
> **Genesis 31:6-9**

God took the wealth of Laban (a wicked man who kept changing the rules of Jacob's compensation program) and gave it to Jacob!

Laban could do nothing to stop the transfer of his wealth to Jacob, once God started the process.

When Laban said he would pay Jacob only in the speckled cattle that came forth from the herd, God made all the cattle have speckled young. When Laban said he would only pay in striped cattle, then God made all the calves striped.

God took the wealth of wicked Laban and gave it to just Jacob. And the God of Jacob yesterday is the very same God you serve today and your children will serve tomorrow.

The groundwork for the Lord's abundance in Jacob's life had been laid way back in Genesis 28:20-22. These verses say:

And Jacob vowed a vow, saying, If God will be with me, and will keep me in this way that I go, and will give me bread to eat, and raiment to put on,

So that I come again to my father's house in peace; then shall the Lord be my God:

And this stone, which I have set for a pillar, shall be God's house: and of all that thou shalt give me I will surely *give* the tenth unto thee.

Jacob clearly covenanted with God that if He would bless him, then surely he (Jacob) would give a tenth of all he received back to God.

Many people construe this vow to mean that Jacob would then begin to tithe, but that simply is not the case. In the book of Hebrews, we see that Israel (Jacob's new name) had tithed in the loins of Abraham.

And verily they that are of the sons of Levi, who receive the office of the priesthood, have a commandment to *take* tithes of the people according to the law, that is, of their brethren, though they come out of the loins of Abraham.

Hebrews 7:5

All of the seed of Abraham were already tithers. Jacob's promise to God was not that he would become a tither after God blessed him — he was already tithing! Remember, Jacob was the one of Isaac's sons who sought after the things of God. Surely, he was a tither from his early years.

Jacob told God he would *"give"* Him ten %. The tithe is not something we *give* to God; it is something we owe to God, for it is *His* to take.

> **And all the tithe of the land, whether of the seed of the land, or of the fruit of the tree, is the Lord's: it is holy unto the Lord.**
>
> **Leviticus 27:30**

Jacob was vowing with God to "give" him ten % *over* and above his tithe, in appreciation for the abundant blessings of God.

He established a generous measure of return from God by the generous measure of the offerings he gave to God over and above the tithe. And immediately, because his faithful tithe had already opened the windows of heaven to him, God poured out a blessing to Jacob according to the measure of his abundant offering. Jacob's offering, not his tithe, determined the amount God returned to him:

> **Give, and it shall be given unto you; good measure, pressed down, and shaken together, and running over, shall men give into your bosom. *For with the same measure that ye mete withal it shall be measured to you again.***
>
> **Luke 6:38**

Jacob was fortunate to live in a *special period of time* when God was releasing great portions of the wealth of the wicked to the just, for Jacob's sons were the beginning of the twelve tribes of Israel, and they needed to be established.

Abram also operated in a special cycle, a *special period of time* when riches poured forth from the coffers of the wicked to the coffers of the just.

Isaac operated in a similar *special period of time.*

The Bible says that it happened to Abram! It happened to Isaac! It happened to Jacob!

Each one of these great men of God saw the wealth (hard assets) of the wicked transferred from the wicked and placed into his hands.

The same amazing process happened again right at the beginning of the Christian era.

Did you know when, in the last 1900 years, God took the greatest amount of the wealth of the wicked and gave that wealth to His sons and daughters to spread the Gospel throughout the entire world?

It happened during the reign of Constantine the Great, ruler of both the eastern and western Roman Empires from 312 to 337 A.D. In the early part of his life, Constantine slaughtered Christians and fed them to the lions. Surely he qualified as a wicked man at the helm of a very wicked nation.

But one day God, in His grace, gave this ruthless murderer a vision in the sky, and instructed him to go and conquer in the name of God.

Virtually overnight the greater part of the world entered into Christianity.

Virtually overnight the great *wealth of the Roman Empire started to flow into the hands of the Christians.*

Oh, maybe it was not the tongue-talking, devil-chasing, on-fire Christianity of the early apostles, but God still gave the wealth of the wicked to His children!

In 313 A.D., Constantine issued a law that would change the course of human history, the Edict of Milan, which for the first time legalized Christianity in the Roman Empire. *All* the power of Rome suddenly became the *power of the Church!*

Every part of the known world was touched by this "new doctrine" of Jesus Christ and His willingness to save sinners. The wealth and resources of the Roman Empire were now at the disposal of the church.

You will be glad to know that on his deathbed, in 337 A.D. Constantine himself finally became a Christian!

Now, notice very carefully that with the transfer of the wealth of the Roman Empire to Christianity, the objection that many well-meaning, uninformed critics of this message bring up is put to rest. They say: "These Scriptures of the transfer of the wicked's wealth are purely Old Testament, and do not apply to New Testament times."

I leave the decision up to you.

Is 313 A.D. New Testament times or not?

Surely it is, and with this great event this concept jumps the boundary between Old and New Testaments, and brings this truth right into our day. Remember, God is the same throughout history, yesterday, today, and forever!

The Chosen People Take Egypt's Wealth!

Before I end this chapter, let me highlight one final, powerful example of how God takes the wealth of the wicked and freely gives that wealth to the just.

Israel was in bondage for 400 years. For 400 years, Israel was poorer than poor. Then God said, "Let my people go." How could this poverty-ridden nation, without a substantial economic base, ever bring forth the great revelation of God's law, the structure of God's government as we find it in Exodus, Leviticus, Numbers, and Deuteronomy?

Let us start at the beginning of Exodus, when God decided to release this nation from the iron fist of Egypt's bondage. Egypt, through the Pharaoh, had a hold on Israel that was so tight and so humanly impossible to break that Scripture refers to Israel's captivity as an iron furnace:

> **But the Lord hath taken you, and brought you forth out of *the iron furnace*.**
>
> **Deuteronomy 4:20a**

In the case of Israel's release from captivity, we see that God used Moses as His man for this great cycle of the release of the wealth of the wicked into the hands of the just.

Twelve plagues came in successive waves from God, from a rod turning to a serpent, to the rivers of Egypt turning to blood, to frogs infesting the land, to lice-like clouds of dust, and to flies so thick that they swarmed until the land was ruined. Then disease came on all the flocks of Egypt, and sore boils covered all of the citizens and animals of Egypt from head to foot. Next the cattle of Egypt were stricken with disease; then hail and fire were mingled together to ravage the land. Then hoards of locusts came, followed by the judgment of thick darkness.

Each of these judgments came with no release for God's people!

Finally, God moved in what is no doubt the most powerful judgment since the flood of Noah. The twelfth judgment came in on the wings of the dreaded death angel of God, sweeping across Egypt, taking the lives of every firstborn of men and beasts of Egypt.

Keep in mind that none of these judgments came upon any of the children of Israel. Now, on the eve of the greatest of these judgments, God came to Moses with very strange instructions.

And the Lord said unto Moses, Yet will I bring one plague more upon Pharaoh, and upon Egypt; afterwards he will let you go hence: when he shall let you go, he shall surely thrust you out hence altogether.

Speak now in the ears of the people, and let every man borrow of his neighbor, and every woman of her neighbor, jewels of silver, and jewels of gold.

And the Lord gave the people favour in the sight of the Egyptians.

Exodus 11:1-3a

And the children of Israel did according to the word of Moses; and they borrowed of the Egyptians jewels of silver, and jewels of gold, and raiment:

And the Lord gave the people favour in the sight of the Egyptians, so that they lent unto them such things as they required. And they spoiled the Egyptians.

Exodus 12:35,36

Are you seeing the miracle here? Egypt was full of the dead firstborn of all living things; there were rivers of blood, lice, and boils everywhere, and here came the unscathed Israelites, asking these bewildered, defeated Egyptians, ''By the way, before we leave here, can we please borrow all of your gold and silver and valuables?''

And the Egyptians *freely gave* all their gold, silver, and other precious possessions.

What a miracle! When Israel came out of bondage, Exodus 12:37 says they numbered about 600,000 men. If you add wives and children, probably more than three and a half million Israelites left Egypt, but mind you, not as slaves!

There were three and a half million millionaires heading for the desert, equipped with virtually everything they needed. The Word tells us that the Israelites were so rich, and the Egyptians now so poor, that the wealth of the Israelites tempted the Egyptians to follow them into the parted Red Sea. (Did you ever wonder what possessed the Egyptians to dare to enter the watery, walled canyon that crossed the Red Sea?)

We know the Egyptians were after the Israelite's newly acquired wealth from Exodus 15:9a:

The enemy said, I will pursue, I will overtake, I will *divide the spoil*....

After 400 years of poverty, the children of Israel were now rich. They had great wealth. *But let the depth of this truth come forth* — God had given the Israelites the wealth of the wicked of Egypt, and yet, there was absolutely nothing in the wilderness to spend that wealth on!

No stores. No shopping centers. And best of all, no personal needs. They had gold, yet they never (for forty years) needed to buy food. They had silver, yet their clothes never wore out!

Out in the wilderness, there was no place to spend money. They had manna and quail to eat, water to drink, and light from the pillar of fire by night.

Now get the *real* purpose for God giving the wealth of the wicked to the children of God. The only thing they could use the gold and silver for (the wealth of wicked Egypt that God had just given them) was to build the tabernacle in the wilderness!

. . . and I will prepare him an habitation.
Exodus 15:2b

God wanted them to take the gold and silver of the wicked wealthy Egyptians, not to lavish upon themselves, but that they might build Him a dwelling place in their midst.

Please get this point, and get it well. The wealth of heathen Egypt was for the building of the dwelling place of God. The value of that great building with its gold and silver, and the precious woods, jewels, and so on was astronomical. But you cannot help but notice the parallel of these former days with the last days in which we now dwell.

This time, God is giving us the wealth of the wicked so we can build Him a temple, a holy habitation *not made with hands,* but one made with lively stones. This end-time temple is not a mortar and stone building. It is the Church of the Lord Jesus Christ made of human bodies of the redeemed who are the true temple of the living God, the dwelling place of God Jehovah.

Yes, God took the wealth of Egypt (the wicked, wealthy world) and gave it to the Israel of old (we are the present-day Israel of God) to build Him a tabernacle in the wilderness. And later on, with the wealth that King David took from the wicked of his day, they built a great temple at Jerusalem. (Both were built with the wealth of the wicked, and both were acquired by the children of God).

In the next chapter, we'll take a closer look at the one who would deny us God's bounty. Can he do it? Only if we let him!

2
The Liar

You Have Been Ripped Off!

This chapter is about the most successful thief and liar in the history of the universe, and how you can combat him.

He is a deceptive, calculating plunderer who moves freely in and out of your life and my life. Every individual life on the face of this planet has been in some way defrauded or robbed by this indiscriminate destroyer.

In the United States alone, he has stolen the joys of family life from millions of innocent children. He has sold his destructive doctrine of "a better life" through divorce to one out of two marriages.

Divorced, "single" mothers and fathers now struggle daily in a desperate drive to survive after the sudden and ugly shock of family separation. They blame infidelity. They blame "incompatible differences" and "circumstances beyond our control," never naming the real culprit, so the thief continues to escape trial, roaming free to rob again! His methods of deprivation include many different forms of robbery. He steals the priceless joys of living, such as the joy that comes from being in a Christian home.

He steals countless children from Christian homes by his seductive temptations to sin. He uses time-proven methods to try to destroy your family. He will ease your children's stress by offering them drugs. He will release their sexual frustrations by involving them in premarital sex. He will even solve their sense of isolation and rejection by offering them homosexuality.

This thief has a world full of tempting methods to lure families into his power so he can steal the rightful abundance God has provided.

He also steals the actual physical possessions of millions of Christians everywhere. He has "ripped off" from God's children the quality of life God has intended for them. Much of the inheritance of the saints is now locked away in his treasure chest, financing the kingdom of darkness instead of the Kingdom of Light.

Some of you may think I choose the term "ripped off" because I am trying to use modern language to describe a theft. My choice of words has nothing to do with modern language!

When someone walks into your house, sticks a loaded gun in front of your face, and then begins to load his van with your color television set, your expensive stereo, and all of the cash and credit cards you have in your wallet, and then ties you up with a rough cord and smugly walks out your front door — that is not mere robbery — you have been ripped off!

I am sorry, but robbery is too polite a term! "Thief" is a word reserved for courts of law!

When it happens to you, the "thief" becomes a "no good, rotten jerk." The act of removing by force your possessions from your life is a painful, "ripping" sensation that hurts deep down to the core of your being.

The most common reaction from robbery victims, particularly if the theft occurs in their own home, is one of disbelief, shock, deep inner pain, and hopelessness.

Robbery is a personal violation of your private life. When you are deprived by any means, forceful or deceptive, of something of value that is lawfully yours, then make no mistake about it, you have been ripped off!

By now, you might be saying: "But, Brother John, what does all of this talk about robbery and being 'ripped off' have to do with me? I've never been robbed!"

Will Rogers used to say: "I've never met a man I didn't like." Well, I've never met a Christian who hasn't been victimized by this thief.

He has performed his destructive deeds of deprivation, taking from the saints of God what is rightfully theirs, in virtually every Christian life I have ever known.

A few years ago, a young armored car employee staged a robbery from his employer that resulted in the loss of almost six million dollars in cash. The theft made newspapers all across the land, yet, his multi-million dollar rip-off does not even merit a single sentence in comparison with the magnitude of the things that this thief is guilty of.

I will not hold you in suspense any longer. No doubt you have already guessed who that master criminal is — he is the devil. He has taken more loot in his reign of terror than ever imagined.

Billions of dollars have been stolen from the children of God as they have marched on this planet in the last two thousand years!

These robberies are occurring everywhere you look. How many Christians have made what looked to be a good investment, only to watch it go bad? How many have gone off on their own to form some sort of a new company, or to develop a land deal, a party-plan, a distributorship, or a pyramid marketing plan, or a "get-rich-quick" idea — only to see it fail?

Just in those areas alone — self employment, land investments, party-plans, distributorships, and "get-rich-quick" ideas — I have no doubt we have already covered an area where your life has been hit and your goods taken by Satan. Every day God's children tell me stories of financial disaster.

Hundreds of times I have heard confused wives confess to me: "I don't know what happened. When my husband started his own business, we were sure it would be a success. He had a good working knowledge of his product, and there seemed to be strong demand, but the minute he hung out the company sign, things started going wrong."

In counseling, my wife, Pat, and I have many times had to help piece back the parts of a shattered family with this type of trauma.

Time and time again we hear: "We had a beautiful home in a lovely community, and Bill had a good job, but we felt the Lord was leading us to go to another place. So, we sold our house, Bill quit his job, and we went, in faith."

You know the rest of the story, because you have heard it before, yourself. You may have even lived it. "Well, Brother John, we just don't know what happened. We had one thing after another go wrong. Bill could not find work. We used up our house money. Our ministry never got off the ground. Now we are broke. We are 32, 42, 52, 62, even 72 years old, and are broke. Where was He when we needed Him?"

I have sat for many long hours counseling dear, precious, Christian families who have lost all of their physical possessions — cars, homes, boats, and furniture — in the name of the Lord! Step by step, Pat and I have had to take them through their painful experiences and begin to show them where in their lives they accepted some deception or lie from the enemy.

So often, we hear from these dedicated Christians something like: "Maybe God wanted us to lose all of our physical possessions so we could learn to trust totally in Him!"

That is a lie of Satan.

Satan would have you believe your problems were with the lawyers, the financial consultants, the business partners, or the deceptive salesmen. He would have you look towards worldly reasons to explain why you have been ripped off.

Ephesians 6:12 clarifies the real thief we need to address.

For we wrestle not against flesh and blood, but against principalities, against powers, against the rulers of the darkness of this world, against spiritual wickedness in high places.

God would never "rip off" the possessions of one of His beloved children just to make a point! A careful study of these situations always reveals some sin, or some lie of Satan that somehow is allowed to sneak into the family, and that lie or sin opens the door for Satan to "rip off" what God had in store for that precious couple.

I have not heard of one area of ministry that Satan is not busy in.

"Brother John, I cannot believe what our son is doing to us. We loaned him — loaned him, mind you — $6,000 to help him get into his new home. We both felt that with interest rates the way they were, that we should help him out a bit. But that was four years ago, and he still hasn't paid us back one penny — not one penny!

"Brother John, he doesn't even talk to us anymore. We are becoming like strangers to him. We have two precious grandkids we haven't seen in two years, all because of that stupid loan! Brother John, help us, we are being ripped off."

I am confident billions of dollars have been borrowed between relatives, and never paid back! I believe that if I had taken a confidential survey when I pastored a church of 3,500 members, I probably would have found more than one million dollars in outstanding debts to relatives. The amount would quickly multiply if we counted the money loaned between the saints that has never been paid back.

Satan is not always a mauler; sometimes he is a silky-smooth pickpocket. But, whether you are beaten and robbed, or have your money taken in the middle of the night while you are sleeping, the fact remains: you have lost your money. It is gone.

The biggest tragedy in situations where relatives or Christian brothers borrow money and fail to pay it back is not in the loss of dollars, but in the loss of relationships between the parties involved and in the loss of fellowship with the Lord.

Sons and fathers no longer talk to each other. Brothers and sisters no longer visit. Grandmothers and grandkids go years without seeing each other. Saints pass within feet of each other without a word, and without even letting their eyes meet. Satan takes what appears to be a simple financial situation, an intended blessing, and turns it into a family crisis, or even a church split, or worse — souls eternally lost.

And what about inheritances?

"Brother John, I'm so excited. I just found out my Uncle Joe left me $70,000 in his will. When I get the money, I am going to tithe my ten percent to the church! Brother John, I'll even give more."

Weeks will pass, but the tithe never comes. Sometime later I will see this same person, and hear: "I cannot believe what the lawyers are doing to me! They are eating up all of my Uncle Joe's money in the court system. By the time they are done, I will be lucky if I don't owe them money!"

This is not an exaggeration. In my years in the ministry, I have seen many fine estates absolutely disappear in the court system, and never benefit anyone but the estate lawyers.

America probably has the best judicial system of any country in the world. Yet, Christians are often losing what is their "just due" in the court system. The dollars Christians have lost through the courts in the course of my lifetime would be simply too large to calculate. And remember, this may be carried out by men, *but the mastermind behind it is Satan*.

Are you beginning to see what Satan is doing in our lives? Are you beginning to see that your life and my life and the lives of virtually every Christian on the face of this planet have been "ripped off" by Satan?

In the movie, *Network*, there was a slogan that is a bit graphic, but certainly does an excellent job of summing up the frustration of one television reporter who was tired of the television station's methods of doing business. He said on behalf of his viewing audience: "I'm mad as hell, and I'm not gonna take it any more!"

This simple declaration served as a rally point in the movie to mobilize the television audience into a massive, nationwide protest.

I believe it is time to serve notice on Satan. He has robbed Christians long enough! For too long and in too many situations, he has "ripped off" our possessions, indiscriminately raped and plundered the saints of God, diminished their quality of life, and taken the lion's share of our assets and possessions from us.

It is time to take a stand.

I want you to use the Word of God to stop Satan's robbery in your life.

It is time to say: "I'm mad at hell, and I'm not gonna take it any more!" It is time to start taking back what Satan has stolen from you!

Taking Back What Satan Has Stolen

There will be no moving into the next dimension that God has for His Church until the saints of God know they have dominion over Satan and can *take back, reclaim, lay hold of, and restore* what the devil has taken from their lives!

Isaiah 40:3,4 says:

The voice of him that crieth in the wilderness, Prepare ye the way of the Lord, make straight in the desert a highway for our God.

Every valley shall be exalted, and every mountain and hill shall be made low: and the crooked shall be made straight. . . .

During the time that this "highway" is being prepared for God, during the end times, which I believe we are now in, "the crooked shall be made straight."

All those possessions that Satan has taken from you can be restored. All those "crooked" parts in your family relationships can be made straight. All those business and personal "rip-offs" you have experienced can be made whole.

In Isaiah 40:5 we see:

And the glory of the Lord shall be revealed, and all flesh shall see it together: for the mouth of the Lord hath spoken it.

The "glory of the Lord" is being revealed in these end times. One of the main signs of this is that the revelation of God is flowing through the minds of His children.

God is revealing to the Body of Christ who they are in Him, how valuable they are to Him, what their rights are, and what their power is in the name of Jesus.

To begin to know how to take back the things that Satan has stolen in your life, you must *first* understand *how the devil works*.

Satan uses *deception* as his main weapon to steal, rob and destroy you. As you grow to understand your enemy better, you will not only be able to protect yourself from future attacks, but you will also be able to go before God's judicial bar and *reclaim* the victory in battles you have already lost! And along with that victory, you can reclaim those precious possessions that were lost to the enemy.

Look at Second Thessalonians 2:8 closely:

And then shall that Wicked be revealed, whom the Lord shall consume with the spirit of his mouth, and shall destroy with the brightness of his coming:

Even him, whose coming is after the working of Satan with all power and signs and lying wonders.

The Lord will consume and destroy him whose coming is "after the working of Satan." Then the Word goes on to describe Satan's methods of operation.

Whenever you can determine the methods of operation of your enemy, what his plans for attack will be, you should take careful note of it. With that kind of information you can destroy his power over you.

When a world-class boxing champion prepares for a fight, he will have a fighter spar with him for months, a fighter who has the same style and techniques as the opponent he is getting ready to defeat.

If the champ's challenger leads with his left hand, then the champ's sparring partners will be those who lead with their left hands. He wants the distinct advantage of being familiar with the method of attack his opponent uses. He wants no surprises.

In the spiritual realm, it is even more critical for you to understand how your opponent, Satan, operates. He is called our adversary, the devil.

Second Thessalonians 2:9 gives you the first key, but you must be careful here. A great part of the truth is hidden from view because of the translation. Now notice that all through the New Testament, the Greek word *kai* is translated "and," but it also can mean "even."

The passage translated "and signs and lying wonders" by the *King James* translators also can be translated "even signs even lying wonders," and properly should be in this case.

Further, the proper translation of "Satan with all power" is better rendered "with all the power that Satan has." Let me paraphrase this for you.

And then shall that Wicked be revealed whom the Lord shall consume with the Spirit of His mouth, and shall destroy with the brightness of His coming.

Even him whose coming is after the working of Satan with all the power Satan has, even *(kai)* **signs, even** *(kai)* **lying wonders** (not true wonders, but deceptions).

It is important that you grasp here that Satan is not the puffed up, powerful prince of darkness that a quick reading of these lines might suggest. He has deceptive powers, but they are limited powers!

All of Satan's power, not counting the power we give Satan through our own sins and ignorance, is only to deceive and bring forth lying wonders!

The primary work of the powers of darkness is deception.

If even an ounce of fear can be planted in your being, then that gives Satan an edge, but it is an edge he doesn't have unless *you give it to him*.

When the boxing champ knows that his opponent drops his left every time he throws his right, that extra edge is all he needs to knock the poor fellow senseless.

Satan will use fear that way in your life. As soon as fear enters your mind, it gives Satan a chance to lead with a powerful right.

But Satan is powerless against a Word-conditioned Christian!

The statement I am about to make is one of the most powerful keys I know to change your life and restore your stolen possessions. If you begin to absorb this principle, this Biblical fact into your spirit, Satan will remain powerless against you.

Life Changing Key No. 1

The only absolute power left on this earth is all the power of God that now

dwells in you and is waiting
to burst forth and move in this world
and change it for Jesus.

That the God of our Lord Jesus Christ, the Father of glory, may give unto you the spirit of wisdom and revelation in the knowledge of him:

The eyes of your understanding being enlightened; that ye may know what is the hope of his calling, and what the riches of glory of his inheritance in the saints,

And what is the exceeding greatness of his power to us-ward who believe, according to the working of his mighty power,

Which he wrought in Christ, when he raised him from the dead, and set him at his own right hand in the heavenly places.

Ephesians 1:17-20

That the Father of Glory may give unto *you* the spirit of wisdom, and knowledge of Him! The eyes of your understanding being enlightened, that you may know what is the exceeding greatness of His *power* (notice power) to us who believe, according to the mighty working of His *power*. (This power is in accord with, or of the same kind, as God's power.)

Pay attention. God wants our eyes opened to this *greatest of powers* that He has given us.

Red China is often referred to as the slumbering giant. I've got news for you. The real slumbering giant is the Church of our Lord and Savior, Jesus Christ!

When Christians finally realize who they are in Christ, you watch how quickly the Church will grow into a new, powerful, stirring dimension. The day is upon us when this present generation of Christians will not have to put up with the things that the saints of God put up with in past generations.

It is time to abandon the old, worn out "God is putting me through this cancer (or whatever you have) to get me dependent on Him" type of thinking, and throw it in the garbage can where it properly belongs.

It is time to drop the old "pie in the sky, in the sweet by and by" thinking and replace it with the spiritual rights, the heavenly heritage that goes with being a child of the King — not someday in the future, but right now!

It is time to stop saying, "Oh Lord, I am not worthy," and start saying: "In the name of Jesus, Satan, I command you to back off. And I put you on notice that your past victories over me and my goods are going to cost you dearly."

This is a new day! The new breed of saint that God is bringing forth in these last days has a way to put the crooked things straight.

They have the ability to take back what the devil has taken from them.

The truth about how to take back what has been stolen has been hidden for thousands of years in the Word of God. You and I have read it over and over, but were never able to apply it to our particular day.

Life Changing Key No. 2

The Law of Retribution from God's own Word.

You can know how to work these laws in your life today, once you know how to apply a few important principles that God has shown me from His Word. Look first at Exodus 22:1-9:

If a man shall steal an ox, or a sheep, and kill it, or sell it; he shall restore five oxen for an ox, and four sheep for a sheep.

If a thief be found breaking up, and be smitten that he die, there shall no blood be shed for him.

. . . for he should make full restitution; if he have nothing, then he shall be sold for his theft.

If the theft be certainly found in *his hand alive*, whether it be ox, or ass, or sheep; *he shall restore double*.

If a man shall cause a field or vineyard to be eaten, and shall put in his beast, and shall feed in another man's field; of the best of his own field, and of the best of his own vineyard, shall he make restitution.

If fire break out, and catch in thorns, so that the stacks of corn, or the standing corn, or the field, be consumed, therewith; he that kindled the fire shall surely make restitution.

If a man shall deliver unto his neighbour money or stuff to keep, and it be stolen out of the man's house; if the thief be found, let him pay double.

If the thief be not found, then the master of the house shall be brought unto the judges, to see whether he have put his hand unto his neighbour's goods.

For all manner of trespass (embezzlement is the literal translation of the Hebrew), **whether it be for ox, for ass, for sheep, for raiment, or for any manner of lost thing, which another challengeth to *be his*, the cause of both parties shall come before the judges; and whom the judges shall condemn, *he shall pay double unto his neighbor*.**

I know this is a very long Scripture passage, but I believe it is absolutely critical that you begin to understand the very mind of God. I inserted this lengthy passage so you could begin to absorb it into your spirit, even if you do not have your Bible nearby.

Right now, someone reading this is saying: "Brother John, why are you using an antiquated passage? It's an Old Testament Scripture that had to do with Moses and that bunch. It does not apply to me today. I don't even own a vineyard, and my town won't allow sheep in my back yard."

The Lord never changes. Matthew 5:18 says: **...Till heaven and earth pass, one jot or one tittle shall in no wise pass from the law, till all be fulfilled.** We are told very clearly in the New Testament that the things that happened in the Old Testament were done for our instruction until the end of the world comes.

As long as there are still some things out there that have been stolen from the saints and not yet returned, then the Children of God can use these particular verses to claim restitution and snatch back what the devil has stolen.

Read these verses over and over again. They were true then and they are true today.

Strange as it may seem, you live in a society where it is often against the law to defend your own property. If you hurt a thief in your own home, in many states you are liable for all of his medical costs, and are subject to being sued in a court of law by the thief himself.

Most of the time, in our courts, there is no recourse for the damage suffered by the saints, and we hardly ever hear of restitution.

But praise the Lord, God has an answer for His children if they have been victimized by the devil! Praise God, we look to a much higher court for our justice!

And with these powerful truths that you are assembling in this study, you will be able to subpoena the devil and bring a proper indictment against him, and see him found guilty and *forced* to *make restitution* to you.

Dear friend, I am praying that, as you progress from page to page in this chapter, you are beginning to feel hope spring up over those terrible rip-offs that seemed to be just impossible to recover from; but now, you see that God is always able to provide an answer from His Word.

The Powder Puff Lion

Satan is not a roaring lion.

Satan wants you to perceive him as a vicious, roaring lion, but that simply is not the truth of the matter. Notice carefully, the Word does not say he *is* a roaring lion. The Word says he performs *as* a roaring lion.

Be sober, be vigilant; because your adversary the devil, *as* a roaring lion, walketh about, seeking whom he may devour.

1 Peter 5:8

The only power the devil has is to manifest himself in your mind with deceptive *images* of his grandeur, deceptive *images* of his power, deceptive *images* of his strength, and deceptive *images* of his fierceness.

But you may say, ''Brother John, Satan has taken things from me. He has destroyed my finances, led my children into a life of sin, and taken away a great job. Don't tell me he doesn't have power!''

Do not misunderstand me here. I am not saying that you just turn your back on Satan and say, ''Go at it; if you have any power, take your best shot.'' But, what started out as a garden snake in the Book of Genesis turned into a dragon in the book of Revelation. My, how he has grown!

Who fed him? How did he get so strong? We gave him this power by bragging on how strong he is. Remember, the saints shall have whatsoever they say.

> **For verily I say unto you, That whosoever shall say unto this mountain, Be thou removed, and be thou cast into the sea; and shall not doubt in his heart, but shall believe that those things which he saith shall come to pass; he shall have whatsoever he saith.**
>
> **Mark 11:23**

There has been much power breathed into the devil by saints over the last 2,000 years. This new power that is being breathed into him by misinformed Christians gives him the ability to do some real damage to the uninformed children of God; *but, the Word tells us we can put our foot on him and hold him*!

We can hold him in check, in the name of Jesus.

> **And the God of peace shall bruise Satan *under your feet* shortly.**
>
> **Romans 16:20**

We need to let our precious brothers and sisters know that the devil is *not the roaring lion* they think he is.

It is time for Satan to be defused and defanged and defeated! All he can do is deceive.

Look at John 10:10. There is a serious mistake currently being made in the teaching of this Scripture.

The thief cometh not, but for to steal, and to kill, and to destroy: I am come that they might have life, and that they might have it more abundantly.

The very teachers who are attempting to defuse the power of the devil are unwittingly feeding him power by teaching that John 10:10 says "the thief" is the devil.

If "the thief" in John 10:10 is the devil, then he *does* have the power to steal, he *does* have the power to kill, and he *does* have the power to destroy, *but*, this Scripture is *not talking about Satan*!

Yet all over our land good, godly men are giving Satan power by attributing to him the powers of John 10:10. *As they speak* of him having destructive power, the devil receives destructive power over those saints who believe he has the power of John 10:10.

As they speak of Satan having the power to steal, the devil receives stealing power.

As they speak of Satan having the power to kill, the devil actually receives the power to take their very lives and the lives of their loved ones. Why?

Because the power over life and death is in your mouth!

Death and life are in the power of the tongue . . . .

Proverbs 18:21

If you read John 10:10 in the complete context, a totally different picture emerges. The context of this verse deals with false teachers, false prophets, and false shepherds who were among the sheep, and these teachers and prophets and shepherds were the ones killing, stealing, robbing and destroying!

If you look closely, you will find the devil in John 10:10-12 described not as a thief, but as the wolf — a wolf that the hireling shepherd is supposed to watch for — in order to warn the sheep. But the hireling shepherd left the sheep and fled the scene.

The devil is not the thief spoken of in this verse!

One of the reasons we have a planet wracked with death today, after immortality has been purchased for us by Jesus Christ (see 2 Timothy 1:10) is because our teachers and prophets and shepherds have been giving strength to the devil by teaching us of his power, instead of about the power that God has given us over him.

> **Behold, I *give unto you power* to tread on serpents and scorpions, and *over all the power* of the enemy: and nothing shall by any means hurt you.**
>
> **Luke 10:19**

They have been teaching us the doctrine of death until it is so ingrained in us and in our spirits that on a certain day we just turn over and die.

You see, when you operate in the human mind, you have a mind that can create whatever illusion you put into it. It will faithfully reproduce a thought, and put that thought into the real world where you walk.

The thieves, the killers, and the destroyers have not been Satan, but you and I have handed our power over to him by listening to and believing misinformed teachers and incorrect teachings on this particular Scripture.

If you believe Satan can kill you, he will. If you believe Satan can rob you, he will. If you believe Satan can destroy your means of employment, he will.

Satan does not have the power to take your life. There are six ways people on this planet die:

1. By their own hands,
2. By the hands of another,
3. By fearing death (**For the thing which I greatly feared is come upon me, and that which I was afraid of is come unto me.** Job 3:25),
4. By breaking natural laws,
5. By succumbing to the aging process, or
6. By sickness or disease.

Look at Hebrews 2:14,15, and as you read it, bear in mind that these verses are further proof that John 10:10 is not speaking of Satan.

> **Forasmuch then as the children are partakers of flesh and blood, he also himself likewise took part of the same; that through death he might destroy him that *had* the power of death, that is, the devil;**
>
> **And deliver them who through *fear of death* were all their lifetime subject to bondage.**

Are you understanding what the Word of God is saying? The power of death has been taken from Satan. When the children of God rise up in the knowledge of who they are and what they are, and who the devil is and what he is not, then the devil will be forever under our feet.

We must take dominion over this world, over death, over our environment, over our circumstances, if we are going to rule in the name of the King of Kings and Lord of Lords.

Do you think He is coming to this earth to *reign with* a group of Satan-dominated, fearful, and defeated saints?

Remember, He is coming to *rule with us, not for us*. You may say, "Well, Brother John, I don't think I like what you are teaching here. It goes against everything I believe in.''

You do not have to like the teachings in my book. But you had better like the teachings that come from God's Book, the Bible.

I didn't write the Bible. The truth is already written in it. Your argument is not with Brother John; your argument is with the Word of God.

If you will read the context of the eighth and ninth verses of John 10, it says:

All that ever came before me are thieves and robbers: but the sheep did not hear them.

I am the door: by me if any man enter in, he shall be saved, and shall go in and out, and find pasture.

The thief cometh not, but to steal. . . .

This passage is not talking about Satan! True, there are places in Scripture where Satan is described as ''a thief.'' If you do your own independent study of these Scriptures, you will find that the only thing that Satan can steal from you in his own power is the Word of God. When he does this, all the rest of your belongings are easily taken.

I do not intend to minimize that one bit. If he can steal the Word of God from you, he can steal all of your *power* over him, and he can easily then take command of your possessions.

Your strength over Satan does not rest in what the world says, it rests in what the Word says.

If you live in the *Word, you live in power*! If you live in the *Word, you rule; Satan serves*! If you live in the *world, you live in defeat*! If you live in the *world, you serve; Satan rules*!

Satan *can steal the Word*, so he is indeed a thief in that respect.

But you need to be careful about the Biblical concept of thieves. The Bible even likens our Lord to a thief: it teaches He will come "as a thief in the night."

You need to be very careful in your understanding about any power you attribute to Satan. He has the power to steal from us, only if we give it to him. By himself, he has no power.

Satan is a powder puff lion!

I used to embellish the devil with undeserved power many times in my ministry. A friend of mine would die, and I would say: "Well, the devil killed him."

Each time I did that, I would pour more gunpowder into the devil's ammunition dump. Why go around kicking a dead dog? You can kick a dead dog, and he will move. Kick him again, and he'll move again. *But each time, he only moves by the power of your kick*!

Satan is like a dead dog. He is defeated. But every time we acknowledge his power over us in our prayers, we kick him, and he moves. He absorbs our energy and power and moves by it.

The battle cannot continue if you stop kicking life into him. Saint of God, wake up! The foe is defeated!

The truth of the matter is the *battle is in your mind*.

As long as you think that Satan is *mighty and powerful*, he can hurt you.

It is time for Christians to let God take them from a defeated human mentality into an overcoming, God-like mentality. None of these phony concepts about Satan can enter your mind when you walk in the greater dimension of our God, and in the mind of Christ.

As you begin to walk in His likeness, and as you begin to walk in His footsteps, and as you begin to imitate Him, and as from Glory unto Glory you are transformed into His beautiful image, and men begin to see the Gospel being proclaimed by your life instead of just hearing the Gospel put forth from your lips, then a disciplined, ordered, informed, active, superior, God-mind will develop in you and manifest the power of God.

One of the first things you must learn is when you give something attention, you give it strength.

In my younger days, I used to get in more fights with the devil. Man, I'd fight those devils (demons) all up and down the platform. I would fight them in the living rooms and dining rooms of my congregation, and out on the streets of the city.

But God has shown me a better way. One day a fellow came down the aisle of my church. He was about twenty-five years old, and was being escorted by his mother. When he got in front of me, he started slobbering and acting like a mad dog. I just shut my microphone off, looked squarely into his dazed eyes, and with the authority of Jesus declared: *"In the name of Jesus, you shut your mouth and don't you say another word."*

Immediately, he was quiet.

When you give something attention, you give it strength. You give Satan power when you constantly acknowledge his presence. Quit letting him run your life. Satan is defeated and absolutely powerless in your life.

But you say, "Well, Brother John, that's all well and good for you to say. But I've got spirits, and there is no sense saying they do not have a hold on me, because they do."

Then turn that spirit loose. The only life that parasite has is the life you are giving it. Exercise your authority as a child of the King. Deal with it right now — speak to that spirit!

"In the name of Jesus, you get off me, and never come near me again. I bind you, and you are bound. Go away."

Do you understand what I am saying? How foolish it is for us to get this vision in our minds that the devil is so strong. Anytime you give strength to a defeated foe, you are making a very serious mistake.

Even the world recognizes this truth: When we give something recognition, we give it strength.

One of the most powerful ways psychologists treat depression is to get their patients' mind *off the depression*. To do this, they tell them to *act* as if they are not depressed (now mind you — just play act, but watch the results). As the patients *act out a state of good mental health*, they find the depression starts to leave.

When they cease to recognize the depression, it must weaken.

But, if a person goes around claiming: "I'm so depressed. I'm so depressed. Why am I depressed? I should not be depressed," that person is actually giving strength to the depression.

Look at John 16:8-11. In these verses we see another stunning example from God's Word of the defeated state of Satan.

The Scripture here is talking about the appearing of the Holy Ghost:

> **And when he is come, he will reprove** (the word reprove is better translated as convince) **the world of sin, and of righteousness, and of judgment:**

Of sin, because they believe not on me;
Of righteousness, because I go to my Father,
and ye see me no more;
Of judgment, because the prince of this world
is judged.

In the Greek Lexicon, the word *judged* means "to separate or put asunder." Now, it doesn't say "put apart," it says "put asunder." To put asunder means to "break in pieces."

"The prince of this world" is *broken in pieces*.

The Holy Ghost has come to convince us that Satan, the prince of this world, is broken into pieces, while well-meaning but mistaken teachers are trying to convince us that Satan is a killer and thief and possessor of great powers.

Satan is broken into pieces!

Now, that's not the fifth, sixth, or seventh definition of the word. That is the *first* and *primary* definition.

If you read from John 16:8 right on through to the end of the Bible, you will never read another word about the devil being judged, except where an angel with a chain and keys puts him into the bottomless pit.

One angel handles this supposedly terrible, powerful lion that has been after the Church for the past 2,000 years!

Notice the angel does it *with one hand*. The reason I say "one hand" is because he has a chain and keys in the other! Also observe that the word *angel* means "messenger," and could even be speaking of one of the saints, not necessarily an angelic being.

There is not one more thing that God needs to do to the devil. There is not a move left that God needs to make against him.

The Scriptures teach that the devil will be cast out of the heavenlies by a group of angels, mere messengers for

God. (Rev. 12:7-9.) Actually, if you can believe it, you can cast Satan out of your life right now, and be rid of his interference in your affairs today.

But what do we do?

We continue to go along, telling everyone how strong the devil is.

He's a defeated foe! He's destroyed. He's defeated. The Word of God tells us *he's broken into pieces*. He is so weak that one angel, using only one hand, can cast him into the bottomless pit.

How in the world can we be so deceived as to think that this poor, pathetic, defeated enemy of God can rise up in any power, other than the power we give him through our own fear and our own foolish words?

"Oh, you don't understand the powers of darkness, Brother John."

You are absolutely right. No one walking this earth truly grasps and understands the powers of darkness. Because, if we really understood these purported powers, we would understand that they were taken from him on Calvary, and that Satan is *powerless*.

Yes, if we really understood the powers of darkness, we would know that they *must* bow to the Powers of Light, and we would immediately storm the strongholds of hell and take the world for Jesus!

But like fools, we walk in fear. We shudder before a powder puff lion.

"Well, then, Brother John, why does he have such a powerful hold on me?"

Because you let him.

He roams the planet **as a roaring lion ... seeking whom he may devour ....** (1 Peter 5:8.) You see, permission has to be granted *before he has the power to devour you*. Yes, you must first let him!

"Well, he took my goods."

Then take them back!

The Word says to hold fast to that which is yours.

But that which ye have already hold fast till I come.

Revelation 2:25

You hold fast to it, and you will not lose it. The devil does not operate in any other power except in lying signs and wonders operating through deception in your mind, *as you let him*.

The devil can only give you *the idea* that you should give him strength and power. You have the power to cast that idea down.

(For the weapons of our warfare are not carnal, but mighty through God to the pulling down of strong holds;)

Casting down imaginations, and every high thing that exalteth itself against the knowledge of God, and bringing into captivity every thought to the obedience of Christ.

2 Corinthians 10:4,5

Now look at Hebrews 2:14:

Forasmuch then as the children are partakers of flesh and blood, he also himself likewise took part of the same; that through death he might destroy him *that had the power* of death, that is, the devil.

Look at that carefully. It is *past tense*. He *had* the power of death!

The word *destroy* is translated several ways in the New Testament. It is translated "without effect," "made void," "made of no effect," and "abolish." It is time to stop saying, "Ooooh, the devil. Oooooh, the devil."

Are you ready for a good laugh?

You want me to tell you one of the biggest jokes ever played on the church? Everyone saw it and heard it. It was on prime-time television. Flip Wilson told us. "The devil made me do it."

I've had people tell me that.

They say, "Well, Brother John, I cheated on my wife, because the devil made me do it."

Listen, Church, he's destroyed!

"Well, I don't think he's destroyed."

Then it is time you started thinking about what you are really saying.

No matter how many things the Bible says that you do not really agree with, it does not change the Bible. Truth is truth.

There will be no peace until you start coming into agreement with the Word, not when the Word starts to come into agreement with you.

The devil is destroyed.

The power of death that he once had is destroyed.

The power of the devil has been wiped out!

Look at 1 John 3:8:

He that committeth sin is of the devil; for the devil sinneth from the beginning. For this purpose the Son of God was manifested, that he might destroy the works of the devil.

The Greek word for "destroy" is *luo*, and *Strong's Concordance* says it means "to loosen," "break up," "unloose," "melt," or "put off."

Let's get to the root of the problem. What you are really saying is: "*I'm more comfortable with a strong devil*, than I am with a defeated devil. I really just feel a lot better with a strong devil. Because, if the devil's real strong, and I'm real weak, when I goof up, I can blame him. I can get up in the middle of the night and say 'Oh God, get him off my back, I can't do it. God, you get him off my back.'"

No wonder there's no Kingdom of God on earth. No wonder we are no farther than we are.

We have gone all across the world and preached the gospel of salvation, and a goodly number have been saved. But, we have not yet begun to teach Christians *who they are*.

We are preaching the gospel *about* the King (Jesus), but we are not preaching the gospel *of* the Kingdom.

We've taught this "pie in the sky, in the sweet by and by" until we have about starved our people to death.

A close look at end-time truth clearly shows that: God is closing heaven down and bringing it down here to earth.

> **And I saw a new heaven and a new earth: for the first heaven and the first earth were passed away; and there was no more sea.**
>
> **And I John saw the holy city, new Jerusalem, coming down from God out of heaven, prepared as a bride adorned for her husband.**
>
> **And I heard a great voice out of heaven saying, Behold, the tabernacle of God is with men, and he will dwell with them, and they shall be his people, and God himself shall be with them, and be their God.**
>
> **Revelation 21:1-3**

As you try to get to heaven, be careful; you just might pass Him on the way. He said He's coming.

But you say, "No, Brother John, my reward's up there." Jesus said He is coming and bringing His reward with Him.

And behold, I come quickly; and my reward is with me, to give every man according as his work shall be.

Revelation 22:12

Church, it is time to lay hold of this truth.

The primary thrust of the Church's outreach can no longer be only getting people saved. We need to enter into the new dimension of our heritage as sons and daughters of the King, a new time of getting those we have the privilege of seeing saved, grown up into the fullness of the measure of Christ.

The saints of God must come into the truth of *who they are*.

We have created an army of babes. We now need to raise them up into an army that can go forth in the power of God.

"Well, Brother John, I've been called to go to China. But I don't have the money, so I cannot go."

Yes you can. The money has been provided. There is more than enough in the Kingdom of God. Satan is a powder puff lion! He cannot stop you.

"But, Brother John, you don't understand. God is calling me to be a great giver to the church, but my finances simply are not yet in shape."

Then start giving. Trust God's promises, and stop worrying about Satan's toothless power.

"I feel God would have me become an evangelist — a soul winner, but right now, I just am not able."

Nonsense. Open the door to your house, put one foot in front of the other, and start talking to the first person you meet about the saving grace of Jesus.

Satan would have you believe you cannot go. Satan would have you believe you cannot give. Satan would have you believe you cannot evangelize.

Start walking in belief, not whimpering in unbelief. Put on the entire armor of God. Get out and soar into the heavenlies with the mind of Christ.

The Church of Jesus Christ has accepted the deception of Satan long enough. Now it is time to reclaim what that liar has stolen, and, once and for all, walk in the heritage of the King! Its also time to stop Satan from stealing from us again.

God's Personal Theft Protection Policy

To fortify our "temples," our spiritual houses, from invasion by Satan, God has given to each of His children their own, personal *Spiritual Theft Protection Policy*.

The conditions of this critical policy are written in Ephesians 6:11-18:

Put on the whole armour of God, that ye may be able to stand *against the wiles of the devil*.

For we wrestle not against flesh and blood, but against principalities, against powers, against the rulers of the darkness of this world, against spiritual wickedness in high places.

Wherefore take unto you *the whole armour of God*, that ye may be able to withstand in the evil day, and having done all, to stand.

Stand therefore, having your loins girt about with *truth*, and having on the breastplate of *righteousness*;

And your feet shod with the preparation of the gospel of *peace*;

Above all, taking the shield of *faith*, wherewith ye shall be able to quench all the fiery darts of the wicked.

And take the helmet of *salvation*, and the sword of the Spirit, which is the *Word of God*.

Praying always with all prayer and supplication in the Spirit. . . .

You are in a spiritual war! Satan has no power over your life, but you must bring him into containment by skillfully using God's *Spiritual Theft Protection Policy*.

In ourselves, you and I are no match for Satan. But *in God's strength*, the devil is *no match* for us!

To be shielded from the devil, we must properly utilize the complete *Spiritual Theft Protection Policy* that God has provided for us.

Notice, I said "complete." God says, **Put on the *whole armour of God***, not part of it, as you wish, *but all*, God directs.

If your house burned down because you built a bonfire in the living room, you would be foolish to expect your home insurance carrier to cover your loss. He would claim your actions were not those of a "reasonable and prudent man." He would say to build a bonfire in a living room is a foolish action, and that the insurance company is not legally bound to cover the actions of a foolish man.

So, too, in God's house.

If we follow the conditions of God's policy, we will stand in complete protection, and in complete invulnerability to the attacks of the devil.

There are six things God stipulates you and I must do:

1. Girt your loins with truth.

You are undergirded by truth. In the world, the battles are fought between large corporations in the courts of law with lies, exaggerations, and evasions of the truth. The entire training of a lawyer centers not around truth, but around the proper protection of his client, even if it means suppression of the truth.

But in God's heavenly court system, truth prevails! Jesus Himself is Truth.

> **. . . I am the way, the truth, and the life . . . .**
> **John 14:6**

Because Jesus is Truth, and Satan is the exact opposite, then Satan is deception. *The devil himself is deception*!

> **When he speaketh a lie, he speaketh of his own: for he is a liar, and the father of it.**
> **John 8:44**

Your *Spiritual Theft Protection Policy* demands that you be truthful; lying forfeits the battle you are in to the father of lies.

You ignite a spiritual bonfire in your "living temple" when you lie, and the price you pay is that you step out of the provisions of God's heavenly protection plan. You open the doors to your house, and invite Satan to enter and take control of your life, and even your energy, strength and influence.

Truth is the foundation of God's protection plan in your life! Watch your words carefully. Keep your loins wrapped in truth.

Remember, the loins are where the reproduction process takes place. Be sure that what you bring forth is always in accord with the God of heaven. Always bring forth the truth.

2. Wear the breastplate of *righteousness*.

If you want God's *power and protection* in your spiritual home, then you must stand right before him in *righteousness*.

Just as we have no strength to fight Satan by ourselves, we have no righteousness except through Jesus Christ. Through Him we stand in the full stature of the new man or woman that we are in Christ.

But we are all as an unclean thing, and all our righteousnesses are as filthy rags....

Isaiah 64:6

There is only one way to experience the righteousness of Jesus.

If we confess our sins, he is faithful and just to forgive us our sins, and to cleanse us from all unrighteousness.

1 John 1:9

If there is any sin in your life, Satan can use it to condemn you, and overthrow your life and take your goods. If there is sin in your life right now, go to Jesus and ask for *His* forgiveness. Through the forgiveness of Jesus, the devil loses any and all ability to penetrate your heart through condemnation.

Remember that God can do a quick work in those who walk in righteousness.

For he will finish the work, and cut it short in righteousness: because a short work will the Lord make upon the earth.

Romans 9:28

3. Have your feet shod with the gospel of *peace*.

This passage is often misunderstood, and even skipped. It simply means that you and I must be willing to witness before the world that Jesus Christ is Lord. The feet are the vehicle Scripture often uses to portray the carrying of God's message to others.

How beautiful upon the mountains are the feet of him that bringeth good tidings, that publisheth

peace; that bringeth good tidings of good, that publisheth salvation; that saith unto Zion, Thy God reigneth!

Isaiah 52:7

Many Christians misunderstand God's command to:

. . . Go ye into all the world, and preach the gospel to every creature.

Mark 16:15

Saints, this command is given to many more than simply the missionaries and the preachers. It applies to *everyone* who knows Jesus, and commands them to tell *everyone* who does not know Jesus that He is, in fact, the Christ, the Savior of the world.

The lady next door that you take to the grocery market needs to know about the saving grace of Jesus Christ.

The boss at work who has a hard time being patient with your efforts needs to hear about salvation.

The person who delivers your morning paper needs to know about the Good News of the Gospel.

Be ready and prepared to share God's Word with the people He brings into your life!

As your *feet* take you from one place to another, and you share the *gospel of peace* with others, you are fulfilling one of God's expectations in His *Spiritual Theft Protection Policy*.

Let your primary business be the spreading of peace. If you do this, then every step you take will carry out the Royal Ambassador's Mission, and it will entitle you to the political immunity of the Kingdom of God.

What I am saying here is that if you walk primarily in the business of God, and walk secondarily in the pursuits of life, you can see God's power and protection work in every step you take.

4. Wear the shield of *faith*.

There are so many things we, as Christians, try to do, believing that this action or that action will please God. But brother, I've got news for you. There is one ingredient you must have and exercise; it is a vital key to ever doing anything to please God!

Paul says in Hebrews 11:6:

> **But without faith it is impossible to please him. . . .**

Faith is crucial to our walk.

Faith is the part of our armour that God uses to "quench" the fiery darts of the devil. It is the weapon that makes us *strong*, that allows us to walk in God's *power*!

> **. . . And his name *through faith* in his name hath made this *man strong*, whom ye see and know: yea, the faith which is by him hath given him this perfect soundness in the presence of you all.**
>
> **Acts 3:16**

There are so many current, detailed teachings of *faith* that I will not try to recount them here. But I would recommend to you that if you have not already done so, it is time you performed a complete study on *faith*. Such a study is vital to your Christian growth.

The Word of God names *faith* as the key to overcoming the circumstances and problems of the world.

> **For whatsoever is born of God overcometh the world: and this is the victory that overcometh the world, *even our faith*.**
>
> **1 John 5:4**

5. Wear the helmet of *salvation*.

Salvation is more than a few words uttered by non-believers when they accept Christ Jesus into their hearts. Salvation is a daily walk, a daily yielding to the Spirit of God, a walk out of a life that was destined to ruin and into a life that is destined for glory. Walking in His will demands that your mind becomes the very mind of God.

Football players wear helmets for protection. No matter how severe the impact from a tackle, the helmet acts to absorb the shock so the player can continue as if the impact had never happened.

So, too, when we wear the helmet of salvation. Satan can attempt to assault our lives, but as we walk in the living, daily salvation of Jesus Christ, we can continue as though the lies and deceptions of the enemy never even happened!

Remember, the only power Satan has is the power you give him when you accept his deceptions. *The spiritual battlefield is in the mind*!

So the helmet of salvation, the helmet that protects the mind from the darts of the devil, is specially vital to your success in life. Through the salvation of Jesus Christ, you and I can echo the powerful words Jesus used when he admonished the devil in Luke 4:8:

And Jesus answered and said unto him, Get thee behind me, Satan: for it is written, Thou shalt worship the Lord thy God, and him only shalt thou serve.

6. Utilize the *Word of God*.

No true soldier would ever go into a battle unarmed. Any enemy would delight in such foolishness, and emerge from the confrontation victorious. Yet, so many Christians try to wage spiritual warfare, and do not even carry the weapon God has given to each of us, *His Word*.

The Word of God is a mighty offensive weapon that cuts down every deception, and every lie that Satan would feed you.

No weapon that is formed against thee shall prosper; and every tongue that shall rise against thee in judgment thou shalt condemn. This is the heritage of the servants of the Lord, and their righteousness is of me, saith the Lord.

Isaiah 54:17

I have had five-year-olds in my congregation who could recite the latest television hamburger commercial, word for word, yet their parents never asked them to memorize one verse of Scripture.

I know adults who can quote stock market prices by the hour, yet never memorized one verse of Scripture.

How can you fight in a spiritual war if you leave your weapon at home?

As for God, his way is perfect; the word of the Lord is tried: he is a buckler to all those that trust in him.

Psalm 18:30

Stock market prices will change each day. Hamburger commercials will come and go. But as Mark 13:31 says:

Heaven and earth shall pass away: but my words shall not pass away.

Put on the whole armour of God and you will be able to stand in the evil day and defend your house (spiritual and physical), and stop the thief cold, not allowing him to ever steal again.

* * *

Prayer for Transferring the Wealth of the World

This prayer will help you destroy Satan's containment of your finances.

Father, in the name of Jesus, I seize the power for finances available from Your Word. I ask to receive these blessings so that I may, in turn, bless Your Kingdom and pour my wealth into the outreach of the Gospel of Jesus Christ. I confess the Truth of God over my finances, and recognize that poverty is not Your will for Your people — Your Son came to the earth and died that we might have life more abundantly.

Satan, in the name of Jesus, you are defeated and bound from my finances. Your plan to contain and devour my finances is destroyed and you no longer have any power over my financial situation.

Father, You have given Your children power to gain wealth in order that they may establish Your new covenant on the earth. The Scriptures clearly state that You have laid up the wealth of the world for Your children. I thank You that in the same measure that I give to You, it will be given back to me; good measure, pressed down and shaken together, and running over will men give to me. Amen.

Prayer for the Return of Stolen Property

This prayer has been written so that you may have wisdom in recognizing and defeating Satan's attempts to rob you.

Father, Your Word clearly states that the battle that Your children fight is not against flesh and blood or human beings, but it is against principalities and rulers of the darkness of this world. I confess the Scriptures over my life and pray, as You have promised, that the eyes of my understanding will be enlightened so that I may know my place and power in Jesus Christ.

Satan, through the name of Jesus Christ you are defeated. I have the power of the God of peace and I crush you under my feet. My Heavenly Father has given me power to tread on serpents, and I have all power over you. I tell you now that you can no longer steal, rob, or destroy my property. Your past victories over my goods are over! The Word of God has a plan for restitution. I command you to restore what you have stolen from me according to Exodus 22:1-9. Satan, you have no place in my life!

I put on the whole armor of God, so that I can stand against the tricks and traps of the devil. In the name of Jesus, I release the evil spirits that are assigned to my life and bind them from any future attack on me. I am taking back what Satan has stolen from me.

Father, I thank You in advance for the mighty work which You will perform and for the faith to stand for it. I speak words of life, and not death, into my situation. I thank You for the power of Your Word.

You have broken Satan's hold over your goods. Now, he must follow God's plan of restitution.

Part II
God's Plan: Tithes, Offerings and Laws of the Harvest

3
Tithes and Giving

God — the Greatest Giver

God has always been a great giver!

For by grace are ye saved through faith; and that not of yourselves: *it is the gift of God:* Not of works, lest any man should boast.

Ephesians 2:8,9

Y ou see, it is God's nature to give. *God the Father freely gives us all things!* Our very salvation is a free gift from God.

He that spared not his own Son, but delivered him up for us all, how shall he not with him also *freely give us all things?*

Romans 8:32

Notice that God wants to give us "all things" — not just those things that are spiritual, or heavenly, but all things! That includes money for food, clothes, rent, gas, and even something left over for entertainment.

All things.

If we realize that God did not withhold His own Son (nothing was more precious than His own Son, Jesus), then it is not difficult to understand that God will give us *all* things. If we can focus on the greatest Gift, Jesus Christ — and the fact that He has already been given to us — then no lands, houses, treasures, or any other good thing we need will be withheld from us.

Even the Holy Ghost is freely given to all who ask for Him:

> **If ye then, being evil, know how to give good gifts unto your children: how much more shall your heavenly Father *give the Holy Spirit to them that ask him?***
>
> **Luke 11:13**

Let this concept sink into your spirit. Our God is a giving God! He desires to give us *all things:*

> **According as his divine power hath given unto us *all things* that pertain unto life and godliness. . . .**
>
> **2 Peter 1:3**

God is the Supreme Giver of the universe. He gives to us according to His divine power! He desires that we have all things that pertain to life and godliness. Get that truth into your spirit and force out any thoughts that do not come into conformity with this promise from God!

God Wants You To Be Like Him!

Man is created in the image of God, but Satan changed that image when mankind fell into sin. But those who accept Jesus Christ are restored and brought into the image of God once again. Yes, God wants you to be like Him! He literally envisions you like Himself:

> **. . . as he** (Jesus) **is, so are we in this world.**
>
> **1 John 4:17**

You know that God is a giver.
You know that Jesus is a giver.

And, you know that the Holy Spirit is a giver.

Now, it is important for you to understand that God wants *you* to be a giver! Jesus constantly urged His disciples to give:

1. He told them to give to all who ask. (Luke 6:30.)

2. He told them that they received freely, and freely they should give. (Matt. 10:8.)

3. He urged them to give the people food to eat. (Luke 9:13.)

4. He taught, "Give, and it shall be given unto you." (Luke 6:38.)

5. He urged us to give to the poor. (Mark 14:7.)

Jesus lived a lifestyle of giving. He said:

. . . I am come that they might have life, and that they might have it more abundantly.

John 10:10

Yes, God wants you and me to be like His Son, Jesus — not just in a future life when we will be like Him, but right now, by imitating Him.

You can start by taking hold of His wonderful characteristic of giving. Begin to see yourself as a great giver too. The giving of Jesus Christ went into every realm. When He met the depressed, He *gave* them a light heart; when He came across the hungry, He *gave* them food to eat; when He encountered the naked, He *gave* them clothes to wear.

Jesus *gave* and *gave* and *gave* and *gave*.

Finally, He made the ultimate sacrifice — He *gave* His life, so we could have eternal life!

You may never be called upon to give your life's blood for another person; but, starting today, you can literally become a giver of every good thing needed by those around you.

Remember that with each act of giving, you will receive; so that one day, if you continue in faithful giving, you will have enough to give in every way God desires.

Remember: you are becoming like God — not all at once, but step by step, progressively, from glory to glory.

Give Joyfully, Reap Abundantly

God freely gives His gifts to us. Our salvation comes to us freely. The Holy Spirit is given freely. And the gifts of the Spirit are given freely.

God expects from us the same willingness to give freely:

...so let him give; not grudgingly, or of necessity: for *God loveth a cheerful giver*.
2 Corinthians 9:7

The next time you write out a check to your local church or favorite ministry, remember that the Lord desires you to give with a "cheerful" heart. Sing a sacred song as you write out that check. Think of the joy your money will bring to the lives of those who will be saved or delivered through it. Put a big smile on your face when you drop your next offering into the collection basket.

As you give with your cheerful heart, remember that you must also give abundantly if you want to reap abundantly:

But this I say, He which soweth sparingly shall reap also sparingly; and he which soweth bountifully shall reap also bountifully.
2 Corinthians 9:6

At first, this scripture may seem a bit unfair. You could easily be thinking: "But, Brother John, I don't have a lot to give. I have only a small amount of money each week that I can give to God's work. I guess that means that I will reap sparingly."

That is not true!

Remember the poor widow with the two mites? Jesus said she gave *more* than all the rich men in the temple. Why? Because, by her giving in proportion to her income, she made a much greater sacrifice than anyone else! Jesus saw her heart. The poor widow gave "bountifully," and God rewarded her bountifully. Remember: "with the same measure" you give, God will give back to you again.

When you give "bountifully" from your own supply of money, keep in mind that it is the *proportion* of the whole amount that you give — not the amount itself — which determines whether your gift is bountiful. Give with a "cheerful heart": God will abundantly bless you.

So do not be discouraged if your offerings to God are not as much as you would like them to be. God looks at your offerings in relation to how much you have left after you give.

Giving
Always Results in Receiving

Memorize the title of this study. It is a vital principle of biblical economics:

Giving Always Results in Receiving!

No exceptions. You have God's Word on it:

> **Give, and it shall be given unto you; *good measure, pressed down, and shaken together,* and *running over,* shall men give into your bosom. For with the same measure that ye mete withal** (measure) **it shall be measured to you *again.***
>
> **Luke 6:38**

Look closely at these *key points:*

1. God promises to return your gift to you. He says *you will receive* a "good measure," literally "running over." God will abundantly bless you when you give to Him.

2. God says that your blessings will come from "men" who shall give "into your bosom." God uses people, and so He has no difficulty blessing you from *unexpected* places. The source God uses isn't important; what is vital is that you understand the biblical principle — when you give, you will receive a return.

3. By the same measure you give, you will receive. Remember: the "measure" is not *how much* you give, but how much you give *in proportion to your income.* This scripture does not promise that if you give five dollars, you will receive five dollars in return. It says that if you give five dollars and that sum is simply casual pocket money, then you will not receive a very big "measure" in return. You will receive the five dollars back, but not in a greatly multiplied measure.

But, if that five dollars is a very critical part of your remaining funds, a precious seed out of your limited remaining resources — then it becomes a "great measure" in God's eyes, and you will receive a "great measure" in return from Him; your gift will be greatly multiplied.

When you become a giver, you automatically move yourself into the realm of a receiver. There are no exceptions to this rule. However, there are levels of receiving: **. . . some thirty, and some sixty, and some an hundred** (fold) (Mark 4:8). The measure you use in giving will determine the measure that will be applied to you in receiving. No matter with what measure your gift is made, when you give to God, you *will* receive a return on your giving: **Give, and it shall be given unto you...**(Luke 6:38).

Remember:

Be not deceived (don't be fooled): **God is not mocked** (He cannot be fooled); **for whatsoever a man soweth, that shall he also reap.**

Galatians 6:7

Do not forget it! Giving always results in receiving.

Giving Is Your God-Given Right

Look again at Luke 6:38:

Give, and it shall be given unto you; good measure, pressed down, and shaken together, and running over, shall men give into your bosom. For with the same measure that ye mete withal (measure) **it shall be measured to you again.**

These promises are not restricted to any particular group of saints; it is every saint's right to claim them, if he or she puts into action God's principle of giving.

Day by day your mind is being transformed, precept upon precept, line upon line, until you come to fully understand what a joy and a God-given right it is for you to be a giver.

Imagine that your local bank promised you that every time you wrote a check, it would credit your account with "more than enough" funds to cover the draft. Surely you would consider yourself a very fortunate person. At first, you would probably be a bit cautious, and write checks for moderate amounts. But, as the bank proved itself faithful and honored your checks again and again, putting more and more money into your account, you would soon realize that this wonderful new relationship was opening up a whole new life to you and your loved ones. Not only would it be a blessing to you, but any neighbor or friend who found out about your bank would want the "right" to the same sort of account. It would be wrong for your bank to offer this program to you alone.

Of course, we know that banks don't operate this way; but God clearly declares that He does!

He promises to give us back more than we give, and He guarantees this return to all His "depositors" (all those who give to His work). When I say "all," I mean *all!* God declares in His Word that He is no respector of persons. More than once He promises that we will receive in return *more than we give* — every single time!

Are you grasping that truth?

Since the entire resources of the universe are at His creative disposal, our heavenly Father will never run out of funds. He will always be able to meet His promise of giving back to us more than we give to Him.

Do you see what this message is doing to your thinking about giving to God? Giving to Him is not an obligation — it is an *opportunity* to put God's biblical principles into action! It is a chance to begin operating your heavenly checking account according to a principle that contradicts the world: *the more you give away to God's work, the more He will return to you so you can give to His work again!*

> **Yes, God will give you much so that you can give away much...**
> **2 Corinthians 9:11** TLB

If the entire Body of Christ began to operate in accordance with this biblical principle, we would witness the abundance Moses experienced in the book of Exodus. His people were so willing to give to build the sanctuary that Moses finally had to stop the giving.

...Let neither man nor woman make any more work for the offering of the sanctuary. So the people were restrained from bringing.

For the stuff they had was sufficient for all the work to make it, and *too much.*

Exodus 36:6,7

Begin to grasp your God-given right of giving. Act upon God's promise to return to you more than you give. If you will do so, there will come a day when the abundance of God will literally overtake you. You will have enough money to fulfill every desire to give to God, with plenty left over to meet your every need and desire.

God's Will for You
— More Than Enough

When you give to God, your gift allows God the opportunity to bless you, to keep His promises, and to give you more than enough. By your faithful obedience in giving your tithes and offerings, you set into motion God's biblical principles of economics. Your precious gifts unleash God's power in several areas of your life.

1. Your gift will prosper you. God promises that when you are a giver, your gift will increase and multiply:

A gift...whithersoever it turneth, it prospereth.

Proverbs 17:8

2. Your gift will provide you a place in life, and will bring you before "great" (godly) men in society:

A man's gift maketh room for him, and bringeth him before great men.

Proverbs 18:16

3. Your gift will even bring you friends:

...every man is a friend to him that giveth gifts.

Proverbs 19:6

This does not advocate buying friends with your money. It simply means that your giving sets up a magnetism that draws others to you.

4. Your gift will stop anger that is focused against you:

A gift in secret pacifieth anger...

Proverbs 21:14

Just for fun, try this when someone is angry with you: send that person a secret gift and watch his or her anger quieten. Don't ask me how it works, I don't know. But it does work, for I have seen it do so again and again.

Do you understand what God intends to do to your life when you give?

When you are a cheerful giver, God will bless you and give you back many blessings!

God cares about *you,* and He ministers to you in many areas when you unleash the biblical process of giving. Not only does He minister to you in the area of finances, He also ministers to you spiritually, and to those around you. Being a great giver produces a positive, cooperative atmosphere all around you!

Giving Will Spread the Gospel

As we just saw, Moses was overwhelmed by the generosity of the Israelites and asked them to stop giving. They had literally given too much!

I believe that if enough Christians grasp the principles of biblical economics in this book and then apply them in their daily lives, every church, every mission outreach, every Christian television ministry — and yes, every Christian home in our world — will scream, "Stop, Lord, we've got *too much!*"

Your faithfulness in giving to God's work guarantees that a day of abundant prosperity will eventually come to you, a time when the reapers will overtake the sowers. But no matter how long it takes the whole church world to come to that moment, you can begin right now to have more than enough by applying these principles and seeing their benefits materialize in your life before your very eyes.

That is not *my* promise; it is *God's* promise!

When you learn to act upon this promise, you can, without fear, ask God how large your special financial gift should be to a certain Christian television ministry, a strong missionary outreach, or to your own local church. Whatever God tells you to do, you will have the money to do it — when you catch this God-given vision!

Remember, giving is a *key* part of your Christian walk. It is not a separate, non-spiritual act of writing out a check. Giving of your finances to God is a deep, personal interaction with God Himself, and is as much a part of your Christianity as your time of prayer.

So do not just give your money without thought or without prayer. Ask God where you should direct your gifts, and even ask Him how much you should give. God has a definite plan for your finances, and He cares about your individual offerings.

Nearly 20% of all the verses in the Bible relate to finances, land, money, goods, cattle, personal belongings, and so on — in various forms — so you can be sure God is concerned about your personal possessions and finances.

He cares about every part of your life, and each part relates to your overall walk as a Christian.

Remember: God is a great giver, and He wants you to be one too:

> **How then shall they call on him in whom they have not believed? and how shall they believe in him of whom they have not heard? and how shall they hear without a preacher?**
>
> **And how shall they preach, except they be sent?...**
>
> **Romans 10:14,15**

I believe there is an answer to this crucial question. They will be sent by those who put God's plan of giving and receiving to work until they have complete dominion over every aspect of their finances!

Giving started with God. He set the example, He demonstrated how to give, and He has determined the rewards of giving.

If you are uncomfortable with any of the concepts you have learned in the past few lessons, don't argue with me. These are not Brother John's ideas; they are God's!

Brother John did not decide that you should give away what you lack — *God did.*

Brother John did not decide that what you sow, you will reap — *God did.*

Brother John did not decide to declare to you, "If you give, you will receive an abundant return on your investment" — *that's God's idea.*

If this message bothers you, talk to God about it — it's His idea, not mine!

Why are some of us so set in our old ways of thinking that we simply label anything as "untrue" if it does not agree with our preconceived concepts?

Truth aligns with God's concepts, not with our own ideas. Whether we agree or not, God will prosper those who give to His work! God will bless those who give, and He will bless them in proportion to the "measure" that they give. Those who give sacrificially will receive a greater return from God than those who give out of their abundance. You see, God knows the difference in discretionary funds and non-discretionary funds; He cannot be fooled.

Remember: that's not my idea — it's God's!

All I am doing is reporting to you in context the verses of Scripture many preachers ignore because of the controversy and turmoil they produce among the carnal-minded "saints"!

The verses that talk about God's desire for you to prosper and be successful did not come from a recent, revised edition of the Bible! They were not just uncovered in the Dead Sea scrolls. The verses you are reading have been in the Bible since it was first inspired by the Holy Ghost to those who wrote it.

Because the verses pertaining to the finances of the saints have not been properly applied over the past 2,000 years, the Church of God is now weak, anemic, under-financed, and must beg each week for the funds to keep going; then it must spend those hard-earned tithes and offerings on mortgage payments while the world cries for spiritual ministry.

That's not what God intended.

Here is the challenge. If you will apply God's principles of Biblical economics in your own life, if you will muster the courage to unleash the process by giving, then your finances will be blessed abundantly, and God's Church will begin to grow beyond anything we can imagine.

Ministers will be trained and sent forth, because there will be "more than enough" money to send them.

Television programs will beam the Gospel around the world, because there will be "more than enough" money to buy the air time.

Churches will expand to hold the ever-increasing numbers of people attracted by the "new" Christians who always have "more than enough," even in the midst of "famine"!

This is exactly what John had in mind when he expressed his wonderful wish for each of us in 3 John 2:

> **Beloved, I wish above all things that thou mayest prosper and be in health, even as thy soul prospereth.**

You have two choices: 1) You can hold onto your old, traditional beliefs and continue to struggle from paycheck to paycheck. 2) You can *apply* God's economic principles in your own life, and cheerfully give in "good measure."

If every person who reads this book will choose the second option, and begin to freely and joyfully give of his or her finances in *"good measure,"* soon preachers and ministries all over the world will be screaming:

"Stop! Stop! We have enough! The end-time harvest is now assured."

And, God's people — His children — overwhelmed by God's love, will shout:

"Heavenly Father, You have given us a blessing so large we cannot contain it! Truly it is as the Scriptures say: There is more than enough"!

First Things First! What Is God's Order?

To understand and apply God's principles of biblical economics so you can have *an active, effective ministry of giving* to finance the end-time harvest, you must first establish God's proper spiritual order in your life.

God the Father should be first. There's no question about that.

Jesus said unto him, Thou shalt love the Lord thy God with all thy heart, and with all thy soul, and with all thy mind.

This is the first and great commandment.

Matthew 22:37,38

That's conclusive. God should be first. There's probably not a single soul in all of Christianity who would disagree with that statement. I do not know of one doctrine, one church, one preacher, one teacher or one Christian philosopher who would argue this principle.

But, to make any *major breakthrough* in the spiritual area of finances, your spiritual priorities must be absolutely straight. *God must be first in every aspect of your life,* not just in your passive agreement, but in your daily *actions*.

He must come before money. If you spend three minutes a day praying and ten hours a day going after more money, then who (or what) is your god?

He must come before your own career. If you spend all of your waking hours concentrating on career moves, taking no time to ask God for His will, then who (or what) is your god?

He must come before your own pleasure. If all of your leisure time is spent pursuing pleasure, reading magazines and watching television, while the Bible gathers dust on the dining room table, then who (or what) is your god?

Yes, God must come even before your precious spouse or children. Family picnics and other family outings assume their proper priority only when God is the head of your household.

God is first!

> **I am the Lord thy God, which have brought thee out of the land of Egypt, out of the house of bondage.**
>
> **Thou shalt have no other gods before me.**
>
> **Exodus 20:2,3**

If you want to have an *active, effective ministry of giving,* you must prayerfully and carefully make sure that your priorities are clear and in scriptural order. If there is any area of your life that ranks above God, then repent of that wrong emphasis, and prayerfully put your heart in proper order.

Remember: Jesus Himself put this order into focus in the book of Matthew, Chapter 6, verse 33:

> **But seek ye first the kingdom of God, and his righteousness; and all these things shall be added unto you.**

This careful ordering of our priorities is the way to bring forth the things we need.

God Is First; Who Is Second?

Like many people, you may get very upset when you find out who should come after God in your list of priorities — you.

That's right. The Bible declares that *you* are second:

> **And the second** (commandment) **is like unto it, Thou shalt love thy neighbour as thyself.**
>
> **On these two commandments hang all the law and the prophets.**
>
> **Matthew 22:39,40**

Most of us are pretty good about taking care of ourselves. Each month we manage to make the house payments, the car payments, and meet most of our needs, including clothing, education and even entertainment. We know fairly well how to love ourselves second, but the hard part is that we are supposed to love our neighbor in the same way!

You and I are dedicated to meeting our own needs, but the Word of God says that we need to be dedicated to meeting the needs of the world as well. Our "neighbor" is every man, woman, boy and girl in the world, regardless of whether he or she is saved or lost.

The Church understands clearly who to love first: God. And, we love ourselves second. We manage to meet our own needs. But, if Jesus placed our fellow man in a position equal to our own, then to fulfill that commandment (the second most important commandment), you and I must be conscious of our neighbor's specific needs, whether they are spiritual, physical or financial.

To be in the center of God's will (and to avoid blocking any of the good things God has for you), you must have as much concern for the people in the world as you have for yourself. God wants *you* to prosper so you can help others around you to prosper spiritually, physically and financially!

If you get these two priorities straight, it won't be long before you will be in the center of God's will, and will begin to optimize the flow of God's abundance in your life. If all the saints caught this vision, it would be only a very short time until we would see the precious people of the world being drawn nearer to Jesus.

Third John 2 records John's wish, or prayer, for our prosperity and our health, but notice that both these benefits are linked to our soul's prosperity:

Beloved, I wish above all things that thou mayest prosper and be in health, even as thy soul prospereth.

There is no prosperity for the soul which neglects the two greatest commandments. We must put God first, and ourselves and our neighbor second.

Remember, the soul which prospers brings material prosperity and health to its owner, but the soul which sins and rebels is bound for destruction:

The soul that sinneth, it shall die...

Ezekiel 18:20

What About "the Church"?

I want to ask you another question concerning priorities. Which comes first — your job, your family, or your place of worship?

Opinions differ.

Most Christians would probably pick their family. But if we can believe the Word, that is not the right answer.

When Isaac moved to Beersheba to live, the first thing he did was to *build an altar for worship:*

And *he builded an altar there, and called upon the name of the Lord,* and pitched his tent there: and Isaac's servants digged a well.

Genesis 26:25

The second thing Isaac did was to *set up the place where his family would live:* he pitched his tent. Now, Isaac was a well digger, so the third thing he did was *supervise the digging of a well.*

Church.

Family.

Profession.

Isaac put his place of worship first, his family second, and his profession third.

In order to enjoy God's best, we must put God's priorities in order in our lives. The place where you receive your spiritual meat must have a top priority in your life. It may be your local church, a radio or television ministry, or a major literature ministry. Wherever you receive your spiritual nourishment, that place deserves a priority in your heart and in your finances.

Since you are now unleashing God's abundant blessings in your life through the *power* of giving, give top priority to your spiritual storehouse — the place where you receive your spiritual nourishment. Make out your tithe and offering check first, before you pay even a single bill. Set aside the firstfruits for your God.

Isaac put his place where he worshipped God first. You should follow that pattern in your life too.

Pay Bills or Tithe First?

To have an *active, effective ministry of giving* in your life, not only must your priorities concerning God be proper, but your priorities in your giving must be clear.

A major question many Christians ask as they begin to put their financial house in order is:

"Do I tithe before or after I pay my bills?"

Many people will pay all of their bills, and then, after all of their financial obligations are met, they will tithe to God out of the remaining money. That may be common practice, but it is not what the Bible teaches in Deuteronomy 26, verses 2, 5, 10 and 12:

> **. . . thou shalt take of *the first of all the fruit* of the earth, which thou shalt bring of thy land that the Lord thy God giveth thee, and shalt put it in a basket, and shalt go unto the place which the Lord thy God shall choose to place his name there.**
>
> **And thou shalt speak and say before the Lord thy God . . .**
>
> **And now, behold, I have brought the *firstfruits* of the land, which thou, O Lord, has given me. And thou shalt set it before the Lord thy God, and worship before the Lord thy God: . . .**
>
> **When thou hast made an end of tithing . . .**

The process of bringing the *firstfruits* to God (before paying the bills) is called tithing. God's Word says that you should tithe first, before you do anything else with your "fruits" (finances)!

Now, you may say, "But, Brother John, if I tithe first, I won't have enough to pay my bills."

Think how full of unbelief that statement is. If you believe that, then you are not believing that the tithe will open the windows of heaven to you.

You see, tithing establishes a new relationship between you and God. It brings you before the open windows of heaven. Literally, this means that the treasure house of God is now open to you. If you put God first, as He says to do, then surely He will bless you.

To break through into abounding finances, you must not listen to the devil on this matter; he would have you become fearful and pay your bills first. As sure as you do, more times than not, there will not be enough left over to tithe, much less to make an additional goodwill offering before God.

Please be wise enough to see that if you tithe and make offerings after all the bills are paid, you are leaving yourself at the mercy of your bills. With this action, your tithe and offerings are subject to and under the control of your bills.

But, if you tithe first, and give a generous offering, then your bills become subject and under the control of your tithes and offerings.

Remember: Malachi 3:10,11 speaks of open windows for the tither and uninterrupted harvests for the one who gives offerings. As long as you have bills, *always* keep them in their proper place behind the tithe. Put God's business first and foremost, and He will put your business first.

What About Paying the Men of God Who Teach the Word?

The Bible instructs a teacher to teach the entire Word of God, no matter what the situation. In this lesson, I'm really trusting God that you will *hear His Word*. Tremendous future blessings depend upon on how you receive this.

Think about the many men and women of God who spiritually bless your life. You have the pastor of your church, Bible teachers, evangelists, missionaries, television and radio ministers, and many, many more.

Read 1 Timothy 5:17 and 18:

Let the elders that rule well be counted worthy of double honour, especially they who labour in the word and doctrine.

For the scripture saith, Thou shalt not muzzle the ox that treadeth out the corn. And, the labourer is worthy of his reward.

The laborer (ordinary worker) is worthy of his hire, but those who labor in the Word are worthy of *double* pay.

Elijah understood this principle when he commanded the hungry widow of Zarephath to give her last bit of food to him, the man of God:

. . . but make me thereof a little cake *first*, and bring it unto me, and *after* make for thee and thy son.

1 Kings 17:13

Elijah told the widow to make the cake for him first, not because he didn't care about her needs, but because he knew that as she provided for the servant of God, the Lord would provide for her and her family.

And He *did!*

And she went and did according to the saying of Elijah: and she, and he, and her house, did eat many days.

And the barrel of meal wasted not (was not used up), **neither did the cruse of oil fail. . .**

1 Kings 17:15,16

The Bible teaches very clearly that the men of God who minister to you in your life need to receive high priority when you begin to distribute the dollars that you put into the Gospel.

Let him that is taught in the word communicate unto (share with) **him that teacheth in all good things.**

Galatians 6:6

The Primary Truth — Giving Goes Before Receiving

I want to emphasize the most elementary priority of all. I almost left it unmentioned, but God said to most surely include it:

Giving always goes before receiving!

The world would have you believe that first you receive, and then you give. So many times I have heard good, honest, sincere Christians say:

"Oh, Brother John, when I receive a million dollars, I'm going to give a great amount to the work of the Lord! You just watch. I know I will."

Well, strangely, the Bible contradicts that bit of human reasoning. The Bible says that a person must be faithful in a little, or he will never have the opportunity to be faithful in a lot:

> **He that is faithful in that which is least is faithful also in much: and he that is unjust in the least is unjust also in much.**
>
> **Luke 16:10**

Now read this sentence carefully: Waiting for abundance before starting to give will not insure the giving of large gifts; it will actually insure just the opposite — you will not give at all.

First things come first. If you want to receive from God, you must first begin to give. The Bible clearly teaches this principle over and over again, throughout the entire book. Luke 6:38 says to give first, then it will be given to you. Malachi 3:10 says to tithe first, then God will open the windows of heaven, and pour out a blessing upon you.

Even unsaved farmers know this primary principle: You must sow before you can reap. You will *never* hear a farmer say:

"I'm not going to do any planting just yet. God must first give me a harvest of wheat, *then* I'll plant my seed in the field."

Every farmer knows that such a thing simply will not happen. He knows that he must first plant seeds, no matter how few he has, and then he will get back a harvest.

Does the Lord give you salvation first, and then you give your heart to Him? Of course not. First *you give* your heart to Him, and then *He gives* you eternal life.

God's principle of first planting, then reaping, is firmly entrenched in every aspect of life, from Genesis to Revelation, from farming to the propagation of every species.

There is no hope of increase without seeding!

Remember what Solomon said:

> **To every thing there is a season, and a time to every purpose under the heaven:**
>
> **A time to be born, and a time to die; *a time to plant, and a time to pluck up that which is planted.***
>
> **Ecclesiastes 3:1,2**

Only one time in the Bible do we read where someone inquired of Jesus how to be saved. The one who posed this question was a rich young ruler who asked: **...Good Master, what shall I do to inherit eternal life?** (Luke 18:18).

As amazing as it may seem, Jesus preached a money sermon to that young man. He told him to go sell all he had, and give it to the poor, and follow Him! Why did Jesus do this? Do you think it was because He wanted that young fellow to be poor?

No! A thousand times no!

It was because Jesus wanted him to get his priorities straight! If the young ruler had agreed to give up his riches for the sake of the Gospel, Jesus would have surely given the riches back to him greatly increased. Scripture clearly teaches this principle as we have seen. Also, Scripture teaches that it is impossible to go broke giving to the poor.

He that hath pity upon the poor lendeth unto the Lord; and that which he hath given will he pay him again.

Proverbs 19:17

Now remember: God must be your first priority. When His priority is established over your money, then the Lord can begin to do some mighty things in your life and in your finances.

Set your priorities.

Deuteronomy 8:18 sets the priority for finances:

But thou shalt remember the Lord thy God: for it is he that giveth thee power to get wealth, *that he may establish his covenant*...

And what is the covenant?

And I will make of thee a great nation, and I will bless thee, and make thy name great; and *thou shalt be a blessing*.

Genesis 12:2

Yes, God wants to bless you, so you can go forth and fulfill His *second priority:* to love and bless your neighbor as you are loved and blessed yourself. God has given you and me the power to get wealth so that we (the whole Body of Christ) can go forth and preach the Gospel throughout the entire world without apologizing to anyone, without fussing and fighting over past-due bills, and without large extensions of credit.

Yes, God has given us the power to get wealth so we can bring the Gospel to the world, without going into debt.

Set your priorities.

Go boldly beyond being blessed into being a blessing. You cannot be a blessing to others until you personally have been blessed by God. Surely, now is the time for the church to violently break out of the poverty cycle. It is time to stop the trickle of financial blessings in our lives, and make some violent breakthroughs that will properly fund our end-time vision of reaching the world with the Word of God.

Remember, along with a knowledge of God's plan for abundance, it takes decisive action.

The farmer must first plant seeds. Sometimes he sows in very hard ground, from early morning to late at night, in the hot sun, often without lunch. If he wants a great harvest, he must fight to get seed into the ground.

The same is true in your financial walk. Sometimes seed planting is very hard. Circumstances may say, ''You cannot afford to give fifty dollars.''

But do it anyway.

Circumstances may say, ''You cannot afford to tithe before you pay your bills.''

But do it anyway.

Circumstances may say, ''You cannot afford to give a specific love gift to your pastor *and* the offering God has instructed for you to send to some special ministry.''

But do it anyway.

Breakthroughs in sowing (giving) always go before breakthroughs in harvesting (receiving).

Remember Galatians 6:9:

And let us not be weary in well doing: for in due season we shall reap (receive), **if we faint not.**

Kinds of Giving
The Tithe...
Is It Still Necessary?

Because many people consider tithing to be a type of giving, I'm including tithing in this section to bring up a particular point. When you tithe, you are only returning to God what is already His.

There is probably more confusion in the Body of Christ about tithing than any other single type of giving. But God is not the author of confusion, and His Word on the tithe is clear:

> *Will a man rob God? Yet ye have robbed me. But ye say, Wherein have we robbed thee? In tithes and offerings.*
>
> Ye are cursed with a curse: for ye have robbed me, even this whole nation.
>
> Bring ye all the tithes into the storehouse, that there may be meat (food) in mine house, and prove me now herewith, saith the Lord of hosts, if I will not open (for) you the windows of heaven, and pour you out a blessing, that there shall not be room enough to receive it.
>
> Malachi 3:8-10

If you are going to receive the optimum God-kind of prosperity in your life, you must not overlook or underemphasize the basic building blocks of your biblical prosperity plan. It is an absolute necessity that you follow the biblical plan in the area of tithing. To get the windows of heaven open — and keep them open — you must tithe. *Tithing is not a biblical option.* The tithe is something you literally owe to God.

"Well, Brother John, that sure takes the spirituality out of giving," you may say. "You make it sound as if *tithing is an obligation,* and *not a free act of the will.*"

Please remember, these are not my thoughts. God says that if we do not tithe, we are committing robbery. He says we owe Him the tithe. There is one important distinction. The tithe is given, not at our discretion, but *because God commands it.* By faithfully bringing forth the tithe to Him, we establish our basic honesty and obedience. (Read Lev. 27:30-33, which clearly shows that the tithe belongs to the Lord.)

However, our offerings are given out of our own generosity. They are totally at our own discretion, and they establish the level of our concern for the things of God:

Every one must make up his own mind as to how much he should give. Don't force anyone to give more than he really wants to, for cheerful givers are the ones God prizes. God is able to make it up to you by giving you everything you need and more, so that there will not only be enough for your own needs, but plenty left over to give joyfully to others.

2 Corinthians 9:78, TLB

Remember: you and I are not being generous when we tithe. We are simply obeying God. For the Christian, *tithing is not an option.*

In Hebrews 7:1-10, we see that Abraham paid tithes. He paid them for himself, before the dispensation of the law, and also paid them for Levi, who lived under the dispensation of the law. In fact, Abraham tithed for all posterity — for his natural children (seed), and for the spiritual children (seed) who now live in the dispensation of grace:

And if ye be Christ's, then are ye Abraham's seed, and heirs according to the promise.

Galatians 3:29

The obligation of tithing reaches across the pre-law dispensations, the dispensation of the law, and now, into the post-law dispensation of grace.

Remember: the windows of heaven are opened by faithful giving of tithes, making this basic giving (the tithe) absolutely necessary. For, without the windows of heaven open, nothing can flow from God to you or me.

Where Should the Tithe Be Given?

There is great controversy as to where the tithe should be given. Some say it should go to the local church. Others say Bible colleges should receive it. Still others want the tithe to go strictly for world evangelism.

What I understand to be the biblical answer is found in the third chapter of Malachi. There we see that the tithe goes into *"the storehouse"*. The context indicates that this storehouse is the place where the "meat" (the Word of God) is kept and supplied to the saints:

Bring ye all the tithes into the storehouse, that there may be meat in mine house, and prove me now herewith, saith the Lord of hosts, if I will not open you the windows of heaven, and pour you out a blessing, that there shall not be room enough to receive it.

Malachi 3:10

Where are you being fed the unadulterated Word of God? This is the question you must answer to determine where to give your tithe. The place you are being spiritually fed should be your local church, and above every other place, that is where you should tithe.

But, the truth of the matter is that there are not enough local churches truly reaching into every level of society to make this a hard and fast rule for tithing. Many saints are sick or otherwise unable to journey to church. Perhaps some of these saints receive their spiritual "meat" from a Christian television or radio program, or a good ministry to shut-ins. Surely this is an exception to the general rule that the tithe should go to the local church.

Now, some local pastors may not agree with this, but I must be faithful to the convictions God gives me from His Word. I trust that the teaching of my convictions about tithing will not cause a division between us. I understand the necessity for the tithe to go into a good local church, because for over twenty-five years I served as pastor of local churches, and I instructed my congregations that if they were receiving their spiritual meat from the church storehouse, that is where their tithe should go.

I never in all of my pastorate had any trouble with any reasonable saint of God failing to tithe. I found that the best way to insure that the tithe would come to our church was to be sure that our church was always full of good strong meat (the rightly divided Word of God).

Notice another aspect of this verse. God says to tithe, and "prove me." God is literally challenging you and me to put Him to the test in this matter of tithing. He wants the windows of heaven to be open in our lives. There is no other place in Scripture that I know of where God so clearly challenges us to test Him and His Word.

It must be becoming wonderfully clear that *God wants only to bless us!* But, He cannot do it through closed windows.

Let's keep up our momentum. We know we must tithe, and why, and now, according to the Word of God, we know where we should tithe. So, let's keep putting God to the test by consistently tithing, and we will see the windows of heaven open in our lives.

Remember: the tithe goes to the place where we receive our spiritual meat on a consistent basis. For most of us, it is our Full-Gospel church. If, however, you are in a church that does not preach the entire Word of God, go before God and prayerfully ask Him to lead you to a church near you that will systematically and faithfully feed you the meat of God's Word.

Can There Be Prosperity Without the Tithe?

God wants to build an end-time temple — a holy habitation of God, not made with hands — but to do this He must have a great, end-time army of very special saints to accomplish His vision. That's not just a fancy idea, but it came to me by revelation after years and years of studying the Holy Bible. It's totally based upon Scripture.

God will give the responsibility of building this great end-time dwelling place to those who have been proven faithful in financial matters.

When King Josiah commissioned workers for the restoration of the temple, he gave the work to those craftsmen who had already proven themselves *faithful* in their *financial transactions:*

> **And let them deliver it into the hand of the doers of the work . . . to repair the breaches of the house,**

Unto carpenters, and builders, and masons, and to buy timber and hewn stone to repair the house,

Howbeit *there was no reckoning made with them of the money that was delivered into their hand, because they dealt faithfully.*

2 Kings 22:5-7

These men were not chosen to partake in this labor because they had *promised* to be faithful, they were chosen because they had already *proven* themselves to be faithful! When it came time for King Josiah to choose who would work in the great restoration of the temple, God told the king to select these men because they had an established record of *dealing faithfully in their finances.*

God uses people who are faithful in their finances, and tithing is part of that faithfulness.

What did Jesus say to His disciples about faithfulness?

He that is faithful in that which is least is faithful also in much: and he that is unjust in the least is unjust also in much.

Luke 16:10

If you want to be a part of the next big move of God, don't just get your finances in order temporarily, keep them in order from now on.

Remember First Corinthians 4:2:

Moreover it is required (not just desired) **in stewards, that a man be found faithful.**

What Is an Offering?

I am sure by now that you have realized an offering is greatly different from a tithe. The tithe is clearly ten % of what has been earned, an amount set by God which is paid to Him as a debt, or as a non-negotiable obligation owed to Him. Failure to pay the tithe is plainly called robbery in God's Word.

I know that is frank and to the point, but there is no sense in beating around the bush with the Word of God. He says it, so what can we do other than just believe it and abandon all debate?

But an offering — now that's a different matter!

An offering is not a specified amount; it is totally discretionary on our part, an amount we freely give to God to establish a rate of return from Him that is *acceptable* or *desirable* to us. By the amount of our offering the measure, or rate, by which God will bless us and increase our substance is established:

> **. . . For with the same measure that ye mete withal** (measure) **it shall be measured to you again.**
> **Luke 6:38**

An offering is anything we give over and above our tithe. You and I are not generous givers in the eyes of God when we tithe — the tithe is simply evidence of honesty. It is simply paying God what we "owe" Him.

But, when we hear the voice of God leading us to help finance a struggling ministry in the Philippines, or a ministry fighting drug abuse in a certain city, now that is an offering — a *freewill love offering to our God!*

Who is going to tithe to a Christian home for abused children? The only people receiving "meat" from this "spiritual storehouse" would be the little abused children in the home — and they do not have the finances to support the institution. So that work, and many more projects in God's Kingdom, survive solely through the freewill offerings of God's prosperous people!

Remember: the principles of biblical economics only start when we tithe. They are set in motion when we give generous offerings. There is a great blessing in offerings, because our offering determines the measure God uses to give back to us. And, offerings are always a blessing to the ministries receiving them, since in many cases these offerings are God's way of meeting their needs.

Through our tithes and offerings, you and I will move into a dynamic new realm as mature Christians, working with God, ministering to the needs of a hurting and needy world:

And they went forth, and preached every where, the Lord working with them, and confirming the word with signs following. Amen
Mark 16:20

The Hidden Blessing of Giving to World Missions

When you seriously search God's Word, you discover there is a spiritual gift of giving. That spiritual gift has many different manifestations. One is the giving of an offering. Here we will talk about another type of giving: specific giving to world missions.

There is a *very special type of blessing* God gives to those who support world missions. Read this key verse in its context:

Now ye Philippians know also, that in the beginning of the gospel, when I departed from Macedonia (on a great mission journey), **no church communicated** (shared) **with me as concerning giving and receiving, but ye only,**

For even in Thessalonica (one of the mission fields) **ye sent once and again unto my necessity.**

Not because I desire a gift: but I desire fruit that may abound to your account...

But my God shall supply all your need according to his riches in glory by Christ Jesus.
Philippians 4:15-17,19

The last verse of this scripture is continually quoted out of context by well-meaning but uninformed Christians everywhere. They claim Philippians 4:19 because it sounds desirable. But read the entire passage in its God-given context. This promise is given to a very exclusive group — those who faithfully support world missions.

The context here shows that God will supply all the needs of those who are doing what the Philippians were doing — giving to world missions. But notice that God did not say He would supply their needs *out of* His riches in glory, but He clearly states that He will supply their needs *according* to His riches in glory.

Now, let him who has an ear hear what the Spirit of God is saying. This may not make sense to some of my readers, but it will witness to you if you are catching a vision of the mind of God. The promise reads, **"But my God shall supply all your need according to his riches in glory."** The word *according* speaks of God's blessing in the same *quality, not quantity,* as His own riches in glory!

God provides a way for you and me to have both abundance and quality. Don't allow evil imaginations to arise in your mind to find fault with this statement. Remember: our Lord Jesus Christ is the One Who freely gave the best wine to His friends at the marriage supper. He also approved of costly oil being poured over Him. And, when He was crucified, His coat was of the very best kind, motivating the soldiers to cast lots for it. In the book of Revelation, in Chapter 1, He is seen standing among the golden candlesticks wearing a girdle of solid gold.

God will supply the needs of His faithful partners who evangelize the world, *in accordance with His riches in glory!*

Scripturally
Giving to Your Teacher

Every Christian has some special teacher who is vital in his or her Christian life. There are prophecy teachers, Bible teachers, pastors, evangelists, and those, like me, who give instruction in the financial matters of the Word.

There is a continual flow of good teaching available to us each day. But did you know that the Bible tells us that if we are receiving a blessing from a teacher, then we should share good things with that teacher?

> **Let him that is taught in the word communicate unto** (share with) **him that teacheth in all good things.**
>
> **Galatians 6:6**

I hope that by this time in our study, you have learned this truth. I do not bring this up because I desire a gift from you, but, like Paul, I do desire fruit that will abound to your account!

I am teaching this concept because *it is the truth,* and only as you know the truth can you be set totally free! Galatians 6:6 declares it. God says that we should take our good things and share them with those who teach His Word.

What a great plan this is. The Lord gives us great anointed teachers to bring us His wonderful Word. After we learn the

Word, we go forth and benefit and prosper from that Word. Then, we share some of that prosperity with our teacher to help meet his needs and to fulfill God's Word which says: **Thou shalt not muzzle the ox when he treadeth out the corn** (Deut. 25:4). God has decreed that our teachers should eat freely from the harvest they plant in our spirits.

When you give to your teacher, you unleash God's prosperity even more powerfully in your own life. You give the heavenly Father yet another avenue through which He can bless you.

What a wonderful, ever-increasing cycle of blessing!

Now look at the very next line of that scripture in Galatians:

> **Be not deceived; God is not mocked: for whatsoever a man soweth, that shall he also reap.**
> **Galatians 6:7**

As you sow a blessing *to* your teacher, you will reap a blessing *from* your teacher and grow into an even deeper understanding of God's Word. Bless those who teach you, and God promises that He will bless you in return.

Removing the Veil from Malachi 3:10

Because of the importance of this principle, I must re-emphasize it. This is one of the most important lessons in this book because it answers a much-asked question by well-intentioned Christians. "Brother John, I have been faithfully tithing now for ten years, and very frankly, I have never, even one time, received a blessing so great that there was not room enough to receive it!"

Every tithing Christian probably relates to this dilemma.

Here is why the tithe has not been manifesting the blessing described in Malachi 3:10. Most Christians are giving precisely *ten* % and not a penny more! When you tithe, you are simply returning to God what is already His. It is not a gift, because if you keep it, you are robbing God!

The spiritual principles that govern the blessings of the tithe are contained in Malachi 3:10:

> **Bring ye all the tithes into the storehouse, that there may be meat in mine house, and prove me now herewith, saith the Lord of hosts, if I will not open you the windows of heaven, and pour you out a blessing, that *there shall* not *be room* enough *to receive it.***

I have emphasized seven words in this text that are written in italics in the *King James Version*. It is common knowledge that all italicized words in the *King James Version* have been added by the translators to the original Greek text. Here is one of the few big errors in the translation of the Authorized Version.

These words, *"there," "shall," "be," "room," "to" "receive,"* and *"it,"* are added words, which do not clarify the original text, as italicized words are supposed to do, but, in my opinion, actually add a meaning that God did not intend.

The passage should properly read: "...and pour out for you a blessing, *that not enough.*"*

You see, tithing only opens the windows of heaven. If you had someone living next to you who was stealing from you, you wouldn't leave the windows open.

The same is true of God. When we fail to tithe, we are stealing from Him, and *the windows of financial blessing* are shut in our lives!

But, when we do tithe, God opens the windows of heaven. But remember: the literal meaning of the original text says *that is not enough*. We must then complete the process through offerings to establish the rate of return out of those windows. After we tithe to open the windows, then we put to work Luke 6:38.

The only giving we do is through our offerings, over and above the tithe. These offerings are so critical because they determine how much we receive in return from God through the open windows (opened by the tithe):

> **. . . For with the same measure that ye mete withal** (measure), **it shall be measured to you again.**
>
> **Luke 6:38**

Remember: your tithe opens the windows of heaven, and your offering establishes the measure God will use to give back to you through the open windows.

If you want nice, simple, easy answers concerning giving and receiving, you will not find them in God's Word. You see, He has created His principles of biblical economics, and they require time, study, and understanding if they are to become effective and *powerful* in your life. The biblical principles of economics are *not an "instant" prosperity formula*. They demand understanding *and* a new relationship with God.

The gift of your salvation is given freely, but it then takes a constant daily walk to keep your relationship with God growing.

---

*Please read Malachi 3:10 in the following versions: *The Berkeley Version*, *The Jerusalem Bible*, *The Douay Version*, *The New English Bible*, and *Ferrar Fenton's Version*. You will find that none of these say there will be a blessing so great "that there shall not be room enough to receive it."

You received the Holy Spirit simply by asking, but if you plan to put all of the gifts and fruit of the Holy Spirit into *powerful practice* in your life, it takes a lifetime of interaction with Him.

The same is true of the biblical principle of giving and receiving.

It is not an instantaneous gift. The principle of giving and receiving demands careful study to understand God's will for you in this matter. It demands faithful execution in a systematic, concise manner. And then, after faith and patience have done their work, you inherit the promises. (Heb. 6:12.)

In this section, you have seen that there are many types of giving. But as discussed before, the tithe is a sum of God's money that has been entrusted to your keeping. Failing to give it back to Him at the proper time is absolute robbery.

But, the act of tithing is the *foundational principle of biblical economics* since the windows of heaven cannot be opened unto you until you tithe.

You learned that offerings are the key to the measure of your prosperity. Your faithful tithing opens the windows, and your faithful, liberal offerings determine how much God will bless you through the open windows. Giving only a little measure of what you have as an offering brings a little measure of blessing through the windows, but a big measure brings forth a big blessing.

Mission-giving unleashes a very special promise *just for you!* No other saints can experience prosperity in quite the same way as those who give to missions. Mission-minded saints can look forward to both quantity and quality blessings from God.

Giving is a spiritual gift which you and I learn to use by *application.* It is *not enough* for you to understand everything that I've written and shared with you in this book, and it is not enough for you to memorize every single scripture I've quoted so far, and then *stand in faith* for your prosperity. To achieve God's desired prosperity, to achieve the abundance that will give you the ability to effectively participate in the end-time harvest, *you must faithfully apply these principles* in your everyday life:

1. *Give* your gift in the name of Jesus.

2. *Pray* over your gift; consecrate it to God's service, then

3. *Release* your gift so God can unleash His *powerful principles* of abundant supply back into your life.

Give consistently. Give when it is not easy to give; give when it is joyous. Give as the poor widow who, in desperation, threw into the treasury her last two mites.

Simply stated: just *give.*

God looks at your heart, not at the dollar amount of your gift. He determines the size (or measure) of your gift by what portion it is of what you have left. If you are giving out of your need, even if it is only one cent, your one penny is a gift of more value than a million dollars given by someone else out of his great abundance!

That is the only way it can be fair, and our God is a just God. These principles make no sense to the world, but they make great sense to God, and, they are making more and more sense to you as you receive a whole new mentality on the subject of finances. Your mind is being revolutionized and renovated, and brought into line, precept upon precept, with the Word of God!

4
Harvest

The Laws of the Harvest

I. Your seed must be planted!

...Except a corn of wheat *fall into the ground*...it abideth alone....

John 12:24

II. You must render your seed useless!

...Except a corn of wheat fall into the ground and *die,* it abideth alone....

John 12:24

III. You must plant what you expect to harvest!

...herb yielding seed *after his kind*....

Genesis 1:12

IV. Your harvest size is established when your seed is sown!

...A farmer who plants just a few seeds *will get only a small crop,* but if he plants much, *he will reap much.*

II Corinthians 9:6 TLB

V. Your seed must be planted in good ground!

...other (seed) **fell into good ground, and brought forth fruit, some an *hundredfold,* some *sixtyfold,* some *thirtyfold.***

Matthew 13:8

VI. You always wait a period of time between planting and harvesting!

> ...a man should cast seed into the ground;
> And should *sleep,* and *rise night and day,* and
> the seed should spring and grow up....
>
> **Mark 4:26,27**

VII. You must maintain your crops for a proper harvest!

> ...and the *thorns* sprung up, and choked
> them.
>
> **Matthew 13:7**

VIII. You always sow *to* your harvest size, not *from* your harvest size!

> ...Isaac *sowed* in that land, and *received*
> ...an hundredfold....
>
> **Genesis 26:12**

IX. Your expense is always highest at harvest time!

> ...a man that is an householder...went out
> early in the morning to *hire laborers* into his
> vineyard.
>
> **Matthew 20:1**

X. A part of your harvest is for sowing again!

> For God, who gives seed to the farmer *to
> plant,* and later on good crops to harvest and eat,
> will give you more and more *seed to plant....*
>
> **II Corinthians 9:10 TLB**

XI. A part of your harvest is for you to keep!

> ...who planteth a vineyard, and *eateth* not
> of *the fruit* thereof?
>
> **I Corinthians 9:7**

XII. Your harvest is a miracle!

> I have planted, Apollos watered; but *God gave
> the increase.*
>
> **I Corinthians 3:6**

All Truth Is Parallel

God multiplies your money in the same way He multiplies the farmer's seed. The hundredfold, sixtyfold, or thirtyfold increase is not limited to the agricultural harvest. The tremendous multiplication principle of the harvest pertains to the Christian's money in the same way it pertains to the farmer's seed. These are not the words of a man; they are the words of God.

The Apostle Paul clearly makes this parallel in the book of II Corinthians.

> . . . remember this — if you give little, you will get little. A farmer who plants just a few seeds will get only a small crop, but if he plants much, he will reap much.
>
> **II Corinthians 9:6 TLB**

With this statement, Paul points out that the amount of seed planted directly affects the size of the harvest that will be produced. No one questions that this works on the farm. However, in reading further, it becomes evident that Paul's primary purpose is not to teach the Corinthians how to multiply their agricultural seed. His purpose is to teach them how to multiply their money seed. He is showing them that the same thing that happens when the farmer plants his seed happens when they give their money. *They will experience a harvest!* By this we know there is a parallel between giving money into the Gospel and planting seed into the ground.

Giving Brings Forth Multiplication

God is able to make it up to you by giving you everything you need and more, so that there will

not only be enough for your own needs, but plenty left over to give joyfully to others.
II Corinthians 9:8 TLB

The traditional church teaches it is wrong to give finances to God expecting to receive finances back from God. Even the most uninformed reader of the above Scripture will have to conclude that the traditional church has misunderstood God's Word on this subject.

Notice this verse is not teaching that if you give a certain amount of money, you will receive back the same amount you gave. It speaks of giving an amount of money and then *receiving back more money* than was originally given. It says you will receive *everything you need and much more.*

Give, and it shall be given unto you....
Luke 6:38

There will not be just one single seed of money harvested for each seed of money planted. Multiplied money seeds will be harvested for each money seed that is sown.

...it shall be given unto you; good measure, pressed down, and shaken together, and running over....
Luke 6:38

If you sow a hundred dollars into the Gospel, you will reap many hundreds of dollars back in a money harvest. There is no question about it; God offers the most liberal of terms. Some of His accounts pay a hundredfold increase, others pay a sixtyfold increase, and yet others pay a thirtyfold increase.

...(seeds) fell into good ground, and brought forth...some an hundredfold, some sixtyfold, some thirtyfold.
Matthew 13:8

It Is God's Responsibility
To Make Up What You Give!

If something is to be made up to you, it stands to reason it is owed to you. Pay attention to this next statement, for a great truth is about to be revealed. When you give your finances to God, *He personally takes the responsibility of making them up to you!*

God is able to make it up to you. . .

II Corinthians 9:8 TLB

That fact in itself is wonderful, but there is more. God always replaces the amount you have given, *plus* a liberal increase! He not only gives you back enough to meet your own need, but abundantly more than you need.

The greatest benefit of giving to God is that each time you give, you reposition yourself for another harvest. There is no limit to the number of times you are allowed to repeat this process. With each planting of seed, you are promised *everything you need and more so that* (the reason for the surplus) *"there will not only be enough for your own needs, but plenty left over"* (not to hoard and stack up, but) *"to give joyfully to others"* (II Cor. 9:8 TLB).

With each cycle of this process, the three-fold purpose of the financial harvest is accomplished.

1. The Gospel is preached.
2. Your needs are abundantly met.
3. You have plenty left over to give joyfully to others.

Your Good Name Is Eternally Established

It is as the Scriptures say: "The godly man gives generously. . . His good deeds will be an honor to him forever."

II Corinthians 9:9 TLB

According to this verse, your giving establishes you as a good man or woman. If you sow your finances properly, it will bring you honor forever.

Many men and women have awards and plaques adorning their walls. These honors are the good words of man about man. I appreciate the importance of these mementos. The Word of God encourages us to have a good report among men. However, it is much more valuable to have the Scriptures give us honor. Your understanding of the contents of this book will instruct you in qualifying for this honor. Your proper performance of the laws of the harvest will bring it to pass.

You Have Something To Give

. . . God who gives seed to the farmer to plant, and later on good crops to harvest and eat, *will give you more and more seed to plant* and will make it grow so that you can give away more and more fruit from your harvest.

Yes, God will give you much so that you can give away much . . . .

II Corinthians 9:10,11 TLB

In almost every church in which I speak, in the seminars I conduct, in letters I receive, I hear the same statement again and again: *"Brother John, God has not provided me with any money to give."*

Please believe me. I do not want to incur anyone's wrath. However, I must be faithful to the Word of God. I am duty bound to challenge this scandalous accusation against our God. *Every Christian has money provided to him for the purpose of giving to God.* Look at the Word of God again.

> ...*God who gives seed to the farmer to plant*...*will give you more and more seed to plant*....
>
> **II Corinthians 9:10 TLB**

I am aware that when the offering plate comes around, there are many Christians who do not have any money to put in it. Please understand, this lack of money does not occur because God did not provide these folks with money to give. The real reason this happens is that they have misappropriated the money God provided for giving. To put it plainly, they have used their seed (money) for something else. They have spent it on themselves or on someone other than God.

There Is a Remedy

The next time you don't have anything to put in the offering plate, try this. Instead of saying, ''God did not give me any money,'' try saying, '' I have *misappropriated* the seed money God gave to give. Because of this, I do not have any money to put in the offering.''

After confessing this, ask God to forgive you; then ask Him to give you an opportunity to make up to Him what you have misused. If you will do this from a sincere heart, God will surely let you make it up to Him. Remember, He is open to this kind of an agreement, for He promises to make up what you give to Him.

God is able to make it up to you....

> **II Corinthians 9:8 TLB**

Write on your offering envelope that you are going to make up the misused funds. Then, as you make up these misused funds, be careful not to misappropriate your seed again.

This remedy may seem embarrassing, but it is totally effective. Try it. You may not like it, but I guarantee you it will work!

Throughout Christian circles we are constantly confronted with the subject of planting seed. This section is not written to present the seed-faith principle as a new concept. It is written to bring added illumination to the operation of this truth and to help establish the proper operation of the seed-faith principle in your life.

Seed Faith Is Not New

Seed faith giving is not only a New Testament doctrine. It finds its roots in the book of Genesis, where every significant Bible teaching finds its beginning.

Seed-faith (faith that a seed will multiply) is the system God depends on to assure the propagation of every life form He created on Earth. Everyone knows plant life continues to exist by the seed-faith principle. Even human beings reproduce and multiply according to this same principle.

The first recorded promise of a savior was made to Adam and Eve by the seed-faith principle in the book of Genesis.

> **. . . I will put enmity between thee and the woman, and between thy *seed* and her *seed;* it shall bruise thy head, and thou shalt bruise his heel.**
>
> **Genesis 3:15**

This first promise of Jesus, the Messiah, was made by God in the form of a seed-faith promise. It would be the seed of the woman who would deliver mankind from the curse.

The Church Exists Today Through the Seed-Faith Principle!

. . . I will make of thee a great nation, and I will bless thee, and make thy name great; and thou shalt be a blessing:

And I will bless them that bless thee, and curse him that curseth thee: and in thee shall all families of the earth be blessed.

Genesis 12:2,3

. . . if ye be Christ's, then are ye Abraham's seed, and heirs according to the promise.

Galatians 3:29

From this early promise made to Abram came the glorious Church with its ultimate commission to bless all the families of the earth. The promise of the Church has existed through thousands of years by way of the seed-faith principle.

Planting financial seed is the God-ordained way to multiply your money. With this said, I can hear someone saying, *"Brother John, that is not the way my ultra-modern, hi-tech bank multiplies money. That seed-faith business is old-fashioned and out-of-date."*

Rather than arguing about this, just read the newspapers. Banks — I mean ultra-modern, hi-tech banks — fail almost daily. Keep in mind that this modern banking system has brought the nations of the world to the brink of economic collapse.

God's Harvest Principle Is a Higher Principle

Before you dismiss God's method as being impractical, please realize He does not think like we do.

> **. . . My thoughts are not your thoughts,
> neither are your ways my ways, saith the Lord.
> For as the heavens are higher than the earth, so
> are my ways higher than your ways, and my
> thoughts than your thoughts.**
>
> **Isaiah 55:8,9**

If you are so foolish as to consider man's monetary system superior to God's, just remember God's system has *never* failed. Man's systems fail daily. God's ways are superior, for they come to us from His ultimately superior mind. Seeding to a financial harvest is totally God's idea, not man's. He is the only One who promises that when you give to Him, He will give back to you — some a hundredfold, some sixtyfold, and some thirtyfold.

The farmer cannot multiply his seed by the use of inside information or manipulation. If a harvest is to be experienced, God must perform the miracle of increase inside each seed. God alone is able to multiply your seed into a harvest.

Understanding Farming
Is Important to Your Financial Harvest

It is important for believers to have a basic understanding of farming. When I first came into the Bible revelation of multiplying money, I knew almost nothing about farming. I had grown up in the city. My lack of farm knowledge was a continual hindrance to me. I found it very difficult to bring forth a successful financial harvest without some basic farming knowledge.

Many of you readers are faced with this same problem. You live in the age of astronauts, computer whizzes, and advanced technology; yet the Holy Bible is a book that was originally written in the language of farmers, using illustrations common to farmers. With this book, we must discern God's will for our lives.

Do not misunderstand. Your Bible is not obsolete. It can still answer your every need. People in the hi-tech age still eat food that comes from the farm. They continue to be born in the same way the first farmer, Cain, was born. They still face the same basic problems and challenges that past cultures and civilizations have faced.

Your Bible contains the answers to all your needs in every realm. It matters not whether it be salvation, child-rearing, or basic living. There is a parallel between the problems of the farmer in ancient Israel, the pioneer on the early frontier, and the astronaut in space. The dilemma is not that the Word of God does not contain the answers to life's most important questions. The problem is that many of us do not have command of enough farm knowledge to fully understand what it says.

God's Principles Do Not Change

Just because we do not fully understand God's laws of the harvest does not mean they are not still in operation. Not one of God's laws is dependent upon your understanding of it for it to work. God's laws operate, not because of your knowledge of them, but in *spite* of your knowledge of them.

Just because I do not fully understand the law of gravity does not mean it will not operate on my body. I won't just float off the planet because I don't happen to know all there is to know about it. If I step off the top floor of the Empire State Building, my ignorance of God's law of gravity will not excuse me from its consequences.

The laws of the harvest operate whether you understand them or not. If you understand and obey them, they will bless you with a harvest. If you are ignorant of them, they will operate against you, leaving you in shortage instead of abundance.

The Truth Will Set You Free?

The following verse of Scripture is one of the most important verses in the Bible. In spite of its importance, it remains almost universally misunderstood.

> **. . . ye shall know the truth, and the truth shall make you free.**
>
> **John 8:32**

This verse does not say what most Christians think it says. It does not say the truth will set you free. It says *the truth you know* will set you free. You cannot enjoy the freedom that any truth in God's Word promises unless you know about it.

Every Christian who wants to be set free in finances must know the truth of God's financial principles.

When I realized how ignorant I was about basic farming principles, I made up my mind to learn something about them. As I did, I learned God's laws of the financial harvest are the same as His laws of the agricultural harvest. I gained this knowledge primarily in two ways — by studying the Word of God and by discussing what I learned from it with farmers. This combination gave me the valuable insight I needed to greatly increase my finances.

Ironically, every farmer with whom I discussed the parallel between farming and finances asked for a copy of this book. That made me realize I was not just writing a book for the city dweller, but I was writing a book for Christians everywhere. We all need to know how to operate the laws of the harvest so God can multiply our finances.

Let's explore these laws of the harvest:

Law I
Your Seed Must Be Planted

(There is) **a time to plant, and a time to pluck up that which is planted.**

Ecclesiastes 3:2

The writer of Genesis quotes God as saying,

While the earth remaineth, seedtime and harvest... shall not cease.

Genesis 8:22

Jesus reinforced this truth in John 12:24 when He said that if a grain of wheat doesn't fall into the ground (seedtime), it abides alone (never multiplies into a harvest).

This is a truth you must understand if you expect to reap the harvest that God promises — be it financial or otherwise. Many Christians live their entire lives without ever learning or fully understanding that "giving" is absolutely essential to "reaping" a harvest. No matter how fertile the soil, no matter how strong the seed, if the seed does not get planted, it will abide alone. It cannot multiply — and become a harvest.

Please understand, unplanted seeds (natural ones) do have their uses. They can be used directly for good nutritious food, as well as making jewelry, feeding livestock, etc. However, not one seed that is used for other purposes — that is eaten, used for purchases, used for decoration, or fed to livestock — will multiply itself for you. It must fall into the earth as a result of your direct effort and will. Your seed must be planted before it can multiply! This is the same for natural seed (wheat, corn, soybeans, etc.) as with other seed — finances, love, loyalty and possessions.

Many Christians have problems with understanding this simple principle. It does not matter how great your need is. It does not matter how sincere and religious you are. God's laws of the harvest must be followed to reap the harvest.

The most popular New Testament verse of Scripture dealing with receiving or reaping begins with this simple condition — something first must be given.

> **Give, and it shall be given unto you; good measure, pressed down, and shaken together, and running over, shall men give into your bosom. For with the same measure that ye mete withal it shall be measured to you again.**
>
> **Luke 6:38**

This same law of the agricultural harvest is also true in the financial world. Without making an investment, not one bank or financial institution will give you an increase.

However, God is far more generous — He doesn't require minimum deposits or lengthy time of deposit. God isn't a fool just because He is generous. He still requires a deposit to be made before an increase can be realized.

> **Be not deceived; God is not mocked: for whatsoever a man soweth, that shall he also reap.**
>
> **Galatians 6:7**

Your seed must be planted. Allow this first law of the harvest to sink deep into your spirit. Its benefit, along with those of the other laws, will keep you in abundance.

Law II
You Must Render Your Seed Useless

Except a corn of wheat fall into the ground and die, it abideth alone....

John 12:24

The people of God often give in such a way that their seed gives them some personal benefit. This is not what God wants. King David was once faced with just such an opportunity to do this.

Because the place of sacrifice was far from his home, it was necessary for David to buy sacrificial animals from a local landowner. The landowner very graciously offered to supply the animals free of charge.

David quickly rejected it. He wisely refused to sacrifice to God that which had cost him nothing.

...Neither will I offer burnt offerings unto the Lord my God of that which dost cost me nothing....

II Samuel 24:24

David knew that an offering which cost him nothing would bring him absolutely no benefits from God. Throughout the Church, I constantly meet people who seem to be ignorant of this important principle. They are giving if it doesn't cost them anything or only if there is some secondary benefit to themselves.

Verily, verily I say unto you, except a corn of wheat fall into the ground and die, it abideth alone: but if it die, it bringeth forth much fruit.

John 12:24

When the Lord said seed must die before it can multiply, He meant it must enter a stage of uselessness to its planter

— it can't be sold or eaten — it has become totally useless to him.

This same thing must happen to our financial seed when it is sown into the Lord's work. It must leave our control and cease to benefit us. It must be given totally into the hands and control of those who preach the gospel.

Unfortunately, altogether too many Christians do not allow their seed to become useless to them. A common, yet sad reason is parents helping children through hard financial times resulting from unemployment, divorce, etc. I often hear these people saying they are giving part of their tithes and offerings to help their child. Please don't misunderstand — 1 Timothy 5:8 tells us to provide for our own. However, listen to this:

> **Bring ye all the tithes into the storehouse, that there may be meat in mine house....**
>
> **Malachi 3:10**

It does not say to bring a portion of your tithe to your daughter's house that there may be food in her house. Instead, it clearly says to bring all the tithe into God's house that there may be meat in His house. Using the tithe or offering for our personal needs and obligations does not let the seed die — or let it multiply.

Give God that which is His and trust Him to supply the extra finances needed to meet additional expenses you face.

Another mistake that I find all too often is that Christians neglect their tithing obligations now with the rationale that they are designating a large portion of their estate to go to the Church when they die. They feel sure that God is pleased, and they have their money to enjoy life with now. However, a person who does this is not giving anything to God. Rather, he or she is leaving it to God — there is a difference. Money that had been regularly tithed or planted could have brought forth a fruitful harvest — thereby providing more for the giver and for God.

If you desire to reap a financial harvest, you are going to have to follow God's simple laws of the harvest. Your seed must be planted without any secondary benefits to you.

Law III
You Must Plant What You Expect To Harvest

> **...the earth brought forth grass, and herb yielding seed after his kind....**
>
> **Genesis 1:12**

It has been wisely said that the biggest fool is the one who fools himself. Believe it or not, it happens all the time. God warns us of this folly in the matter of sowing and reaping.

> **Be not deceived; God is not mocked: for whatsoever a man soweth, that shall he also reap.**
>
> **Galatians 6:7**

This law is set in time and eternity. It is irreversible. The seed you plant determines the kind of harvest you will reap. By some ingenious method, you might disguise an orange seed as a lemon seed and even fool yourself into believing it. But after the seed is planted and the tree grown, it will bear oranges, not lemons — because you reaped what you sowed — oranges.

I cannot stress this point strongly enough — it is not the kind of harvest you need that determines the kind of harvest you will receive. It is the kind of seed you plant that determines the kind of harvest you will reap. Don't fool yourself.

Let me illustrate this with an incident out of my own experience. Some years ago, I was approached by a young man who very respectfully asked me to help him understand why the principle of seed giving had not worked in his precious mother's case. Her devotion to God was unswerving. She visited the sick. She cooked delicious meals for shut-ins. She made beautiful afghans for friends and relatives.

However, now in her last years, no financial harvest had been manifested because of her giving. Just the opposite had occurred. She was now penniless and being cared for in a welfare nursing home.

The young man's painful cry was, "Why wasn't my mother's generous giving honored by God?"

As we talked further, I asked if his mother had many visitors. He said that her room was always crowded. A little later, I asked if anyone ever brought his mother meals or desserts to the nursing home. He answered that the doctor and nurses had a terrible time keeping her on a proper diet because of it. With a dawning realization, he said, "I know your next question. Does she ever receive afghans? Yes, her room and her closet are full of afghans."

When I asked if his mother tithed regularly, he said that neither he nor his mother believed in tithing, that it was Old Testament and not for our day. They made it a practice not to give to any ministry that asked for money. Our conversation ended abruptly.

Give and it shall be given unto you....
Luke 6:38

Notice the word "it." A very large and powerful word for only having two letters. Let me paraphrase. Give apples, and it (apples) will be given unto you. Give afghans, and it (afghans) will be given unto you. Give money, and it (money) will be given unto you. You cannot sow afghans and reap retirement income. Please don't misunderstand. I am quite sure that the mother's afghans were loved and appreciated. However, God should not be chastised for not producing a harvest. He did what He could with the seeds planted.

Don't fool yourself. If it is a financial harvest you seek, it must be seeds of finance you plant.

Law IV
Your Harvest Size is Established When Your Seed Is Sown

. . . remember this — if you give little, you will get little. A farmer who plants just a few seeds will get only a small crop, but if he plants much, he will reap much.

II Corinthians 9:6 TLB

No matter how convenient it would be, you cannot wait until the day of the harvest to decide how big a harvest you want. That was determined back when you planted the seeds. There is always a season (a reasonable period of time) between the time of sowing and the time of harvesting. So you must decide well in advance if you want a bountiful harvest, just an adequate one, or none at all.

I have made an interesting observation during my adult years. It is much easier to adjust to the problem of having more than enough than it is to adjust to the problem of having too little. Wise farmers always plant more than they might need. It is easier to deal with too much rather than too little!

As unbelievable as it sounds, I have heard Christian people say they did not need to give much to God because they did not need much to be happy. By some misguided piety, they reasoned it was spiritual not to desire more than enough. I believe this attitude is nothing more than an attempt to cover up their lack of faith to believe God for more than enough. This lack of faith coupled with ignorance of God's purpose brings men to this decidedly unscriptural conclusion.

Dear Christian friend, you cannot be what God is calling you to be if you only have "enough." You need more than enough to be a good Christian. With only "enough," you are assured of not having enough to do God's will or fulfill the covenant God made with Abraham. Remember, you are the seed of Abraham,

> **. . . if ye be Christ's, then are ye Abraham's seed, and heirs according to the promise.**
>
> **Galatians 3:29**

What did God promise the world that you, the seed of Abraham, would be?

> **And I will make of thee a great nation, and I will bless thee, and make thy name great; and thou shalt be a blessing:**
>
> **And I shall bless them that bless thee, and curse them that curse thee: and in thee shall all families of the earth be blessed.**
>
> **Genesis 12:2,3**

You are meant to be a blessing. How can you be a blessing to anyone, much less all the families of the world, unless you have been blessed? In James 2:15-17, we are told to feed the hungry and clothe the naked. How can you possibly feed and clothe others if you have only enough to feed and clothe yourself?

The reason God wants you to have more than enough is not to selfishly hide it away. He wants abundance in your life so you can not only meet all your own needs, but cheerfully bless and meet the needs of others.

It is so much easier to be a blessing when you have both planted and harvested much, rather than when you have planted little and reaped little. In abundance, you have choices. In shortage, you have misery.

The choice is, of course, yours — to plant much or to plant little. You may be able to plant more than you think through faith-giving. You don't have to wait for a financial windfall to make a substantial gift to God with your offerings. Just set an amount that you can believe God for each week. Giving just $10 a week equals $520 per year.

Determine what you want to harvest now. Then begin planting the necessary number of seeds.

Law V
Your Seed Must Be Planted In Good Ground

But other (seed) **fell into good ground, and brought forth...some an hundredfold, some sixtyfold, some thirtyfold.**

Matthew 13:8

The story of the sower planting his seed in four different kinds of ground is well known. Seed spilled along the wayside and not covered is soon eaten by birds or other animals. Seed sown in stony ground with no depth of rich soil springs up but soon withers in the heat. Seed sown among thorns or weeds will quickly be choked out. However, seed sown into good ground brings forth the miracle process of multiplication called the harvest. In harvest, there may be some hundredfold, sixtyfold, or thirtyfold increase.

Just as this law operates in the agricultural world, so, too, does it operate in the world of Christian finances.

How do we identify the best ground in which to plant? I thank God for every good Gospel-preaching ministry and every local church that operates today. However, we all know that not all ministries preach and teach the full Gospel. By this, we can conclude that some ground is better than others.

The next four sentences are extremely important; please read them carefully.

There are ministries and churches that exist to minister. On the other hand, there are also ministries and churches that minister to exist. One raises money to minister. The other ministers to raise money.

There is an unmistakable characteristic that exists in every good ground ministry. It will vigorously attempt to accomplish the specific purpose given it by God. How do you recognize good ground? First of all, do not be afraid to investigate, to ask questions, to inspect. A good-ground ministry (be it a local Full Gospel church, a para-church ministry perhaps ministering to prisoners, the retarded, etc. in cooperation with a local church, or a Christian television station or network) will be open and happy to answer your questions. In knowing good ground, God has also given us an unction.

> **. . . ye have an unction from the Holy One, and ye know all things.**
>
> **I John 2:20**

With your God-given unction you can discern good ground. Discover the good ground and plant in it to reap the harvest God has for you.

Law VI
You Must Always Wait A Period
Of Time Between Planting And Harvesting

> . . . a man should cast a seed into the ground;
> and should sleep, and rise night and day, and the
> seed should spring and grow up . . .
>
> **Mark 4:26,27**

Faith, as we know, is a key factor in seed-planting. A less well-known but equally important factor is patience. We receive God's blessings through both faith and patience.

> . . . be not slothful, but followers of them who
> through faith and patience inherit the promises.
>
> **Hebrews 6:12**

There is a Scripture that is very popular. It is usually quoted this way. "Cast your bread upon the water, and it will come back to you again." While this rendition gives the essence, it leaves out one of the essentials of the verse as it is written.

> Cast thy bread upon the waters: for thou shalt
> find it after many days.
>
> **Ecclesiastes 11:1**

As I mentioned before, there is a season between planting and reaping. Faith and patience help us through that season.

> . . . ye have need of patience, that, after ye
> have done the will of God, ye might receive the
> promise.
>
> **Hebrews 10:36**

Lack of patience can cancel your harvest — it can even do that in the realm of worldly finances. If you invest in a Certificate of Deposit for a specified amount of time, you are guaranteed a harvest or return at the end of that time period. However, if you withdraw early, you risk losing a major portion, if not all of the interest you were to reap.

The same is true in the supernatural realm where you have planted your seeds of money. The problem is, it's even easier to cancel your harvest from God than it is from the local bank. If you allow impatience to weaken your faith to the point you are muttering such things as "God's harvest plan isn't working for me," or "I don't think God is going to come through this time," you have cancelled the harvest. You, not God.

In the spiritual realm, words are powerful — very, very powerful. Words of faith or doubt can change things in your life quickly, if not immediately. I am convinced that Christians have missed some of the greatest financial harvests of all time. They simply spoke them out of existence due to impatience. In essence, they were saying, "I cancel my harvest."

Keep your faith. Be patient. If you are obeying the laws of the harvest, it is coming.

Law VII
You Must Maintain Your Crops
For A Proper Harvest

...the thorns sprung up, and choked them....

Matthew 13:7

After a farmer selects his crop, decides on the amount of seed to plant, plants them and watches them sprout, he doesn't just sit back and wait for the harvest. He must still nurture and protect the crop until harvest time.

A Christian's financial harvest-to-be must similarly be maintained. In particular, there are three areas of "crop" maintenance that must be attended to:

1) You must put God and a godly lifestyle first.

> **. . . seek ye first the kingdom of God, and his righteousness; and all these things shall be added unto you.**
>
> **Matthew 6:33**

You must allow the kingdom of God to manifest itself in you. Seeking first the kingdom of God is the process of actively seeking the rulership of Jesus Christ in your life. Seeking His righteousness is pressing forward toward the goal of becoming like Jesus Christ.

2) The evangelism of the world must be a priority.

> **. . . I will make of thee a great nation, and I will bless thee, and make thy name great; and thou shalt be a blessing:**
>
> **And I will bless them that bless thee, and curse them that curseth thee: and in thee shall all families of the earth be blessed.**
>
> **Genesis 12:2,3**

The power to prosper, to be wealthy is explicitly promised to those who desire *to be a blessing* instead of wishing only to be blessed. They will be a blessing through the Gospel of Jesus Christ by sharing the Gospel and meeting the worldly needs of the hungry, the naked and the homeless.

3) You must discern deception.

The devil possesses three basic powers — the power to tempt, the power to accuse, and none more powerful than the power to deceive. His deception can be devastating! In the parable of the sower in Matthew 13:22, we see that the deceitfulness of riches can cause men to become unfruitful.

When your financial harvest begins, do not be deceived by the increase in your wealth. Do not begin to lavish it solely upon yourself. Remember these words:

Ye ask, and receive not, because ye ask amiss, that ye may consume it upon your lusts.

James 4:3

Being deceived by the sudden influx of wealth will turn the harvest process around. You can quickly become unfruitful.

You must maintain a clean godly life, always moving nearer to God. Give the lion's share of your surplus to the evangelism of the world. Stay alert for Satan's deceptions, even in the smallest parts of your life, about where your bounty came from and where it should really go.

Law VIII
You Must Always Sow To Your Harvest Size, Not From Your Harvest Size

...Isaac sowed in that land (of famine)**, and received in the same year an hundredfold....**

Genesis 26:12

I have never lived on a farm. Something I learned from farmers may come as big a shock to you as it was to me. The time when a farmer must make his largest and most costly seed purchase is when he can least afford it. This happens when he has suffered a previous crop failure. Money is tight; the urge to conserve is great. Yet the farmer must plant more than ever to make up for the shortage caused by the failed crop.

The farmer must plant more seed, in more acres, perhaps in ground that he has allowed to lay fallow, to make up for his shortfall. He needs to plant for his biggest harvest when his funds are the shortest.

Unfortunately, altogether too many Christians don't know this basic law of agriculture. They sow from their harvest — if large, they tithe and offer larger amounts. If their current harvest has been small, they tithe and offer small amounts. They continue to sow from their harvest, rather than as is God's way, to their harvest.

There is no way to calculate how many of God's children are at the bottom of the financial barrel because they violate this most important law. I am convinced the majority of Christians gauge the size of their offerings by the size of their income, instead of by the size income they desire in the future.

Every church I ever pastored was full of people who allowed their giving to be influenced by adverse economic circumstances. Rumors of factory closings or other economic crises would cause the weekly offering to immediately go down.

For some reason, the fear of insufficiency tends to overshadow our faith in God. This shouldn't be so. We are to give according to our desired future harvest, not from past or present shortage. The very fact that you need a greater financial harvest witnesses to the insufficiency of your past harvest or harvests. Your natural tendency will be to give according to your financial shortage. Doing this will not solve your problem; it will only prolong and intensify it.

Faith-promise giving may be the answer for you. Give what you can now and pay the rest of your promise in regular payments. With faith-promise giving, you are only obligated to give if God supplies you. But remember this, God never fails.

If your past harvests have been sufficient for you and the work God has asked you to do, you are probably planting enough. If your harvests have been less than enough or you want to be able to do even more of God's work, you must plant even more than before. When you give more, you will reap more.

Law IX
Your Expense Is Always
Highest At Harvest Time

. . . the kingdom of heaven is like unto a man that is an householder, which went out early in the morning to hire labourers into his vineyard.
Matthew 20:1

By now you have learned there are many painstaking steps the farmer must take before he can experience a harvest. He must plant his seed. He must plant in the good ground. He must care for his crops as they grow. As costly as all these steps may be, they are not the most expensive steps he will have to take.

On the day the crop is ripe, the farmer must hire laborers to break the harvest loose from the stalk. A substantial cost is incurred before the farmer can reap the full benefit of the harvest.

In my experience with financial harvests, the same thing is true. While it may not be as readily identifiable as having to hire laborers, we must expect to give a special harvest release offering just as we sense our financial harvest is fully ripe and ready to be reaped.

If you have been sowing regularly, ask God if this special harvest release offering is not the key you have been looking for. Put this principle to work right now. Write a substantial check and send it to a good-ground ministry to break loose your harvest.

Law X
A Part of Your Harvest Is For Sowing Again

...God, who gives seed to the farmer to plant, and later on, good crops to harvest and eat, will give you more and more seed to plant and will make it grow so that you can give away more and more fruit from your harvest.

II Corinthians 9:10 TLB

What do you call a farmer who eats all of his harvest? A fool! A true farmer always saves some seed from each harvest to replant.

Perhaps it is a shame that more Christians don't have a farming background. Several years ago, I delivered several strong sermons to my congregation to put God to the test by planting a substantial financial seed into the ministry. I asked that they report back to me with the results.

I was amazed at how quickly almost everyone received a great financial harvest — the church was astir with testimonies. I was elated. People had learned an important lesson of God and had received substantial material benefits besides. After a few months, I began questioning people individually to see how they were progressing with subsequent sowing and reaping. I was devastated! I found that only about one out of ten replanted any seed from their harvest. Not only weren't they replanting, over sixty % had never even tithed on their original harvest.

As I have said before, don't fool yourself. The most important part of each and every harvest is not the part you eat, but the part you faithfully plant again. The miracle of the perpetual financial harvest depends on your ability to plant a portion of each harvest back into the Gospel.

You can harvest over and over again as long as you plant from each harvest. Yes! You can harvest until Jesus returns if you will not grow weary in well doing, and sow again from each new harvest.

Law XI
A Part of The Harvest Is For You To Keep

> . . . who planteth a vineyard, and eateth not
> of the fruit thereof?
>
> **I Corinthians 9:7**

There are those who teach that Christians are not to have any material possessions, or limited possessions at best. This idea has attracted followers throughout church history. Even today, the predominant mentality throughout the church is that God wants his children to be poor. This has left the church at the edge of bankruptcy, and most church members barely able to survive. This teaching is almost totally devoid of any balance or biblical basis.

The Bible, instead, teaches us of Kingdom stewardship. This is the teaching that we (God's children) are to have all sufficiency, actually more than enough to meet all our needs and desires. But it doesn't even stop there. It goes on to teach that we will have an abundant surplus to give generously into every endeavor where God directs.

> **God is able to make it up to you by giving
> you everything you need and more, so that there
> will not only be enough for your own needs, but
> plenty left over to give joyfully to others.**
>
> **II Corinthians 9:8 TLB**

Throughout the Bible, God invites us to eat our fill from the abundance of every harvest He brings forth from our seed. Please do not draw back from enjoying your portion of the harvest because of the misunderstanding of others. If you give in accordance with the laws of the harvest and live a life consistent with God's Word, you will reap a harvest. When the harvest is reaped, a substantial portion of it will be for the express purpose of your enjoyment.

Law XII
Your Harvest Is A Miracle

I have planted, Apollos watered; but God gave the increase.

I Corinthians 3:6

No factory or laboratory has ever manufactured a seed that can reproduce itself. None has ever made a seed that can multiply itself into a harvest.

Only God can make seed that multiplies. The origin of seed is not in the genus of creation, but in the power of the Creator. Each and every seed is a miracle capsule that with proper planting and care will reproduce itself.

Always remember that when a harvest occurs, be it agricultural or financial, a miracle has taken place. Harvest always necessitates the intervention of God. There can be no harvest without Him. He is the giver of life.

The Lord's part in any harvest you seek must be acknowledged and diligently sought after. Your situation may be such that to reap a harvest seems impossible. Without God's intervention, it may well be impossible. Seek His help, in the name of Jesus Christ. Command your seed to come forth in Jesus' name. Let your faith be strong.

> **Therefore I say unto you, What things soever ye desire** (your harvest)**, when ye pray, believe that ye receive them, and ye shall have them.**
>
> **Mark 11:24**

Satan, the thief, will try to steal your harvest. We'll explore more about dealing with him in the next chapter. He will bring doubt. You must shield your faith from doubt. You must speak only words of victory concerning your financial harvest, not defeat. Petition God in prayer for an abundant harvest. Your Heavenly Father will hear. He will act. His miracle, your harvest, will bless you.

*　　　*　　　*

Prayer for Unlocking the Powerful Principles of Increase

This prayer will help you unlock a new spirit of giving within you and propel you into a new level of giving to God.

Father, in the name of Jesus, I come expecting Your Word to be manifest in me. The Scriptures state that as You have given unto me, I am to give unto others. I pray that I freely and cheerfully give to those who are in need. I confess Your Word for spiritual and physical blessings in my life. As your Son came to give me life more abundantly, I choose in my heart to reach out and give to others.

Satan, you are defeated and, by the power of Jesus' name, you are bound from my life and giving. You cannot steal, rob or destroy. As my heavenly Father has given to me, so will I give to others.

Lord, I look upon giving to You as an opportunity to put scriptural principles into action. Your Word states that in the measure with which I give unto You, You will bless me accordingly. I sow bountifully so that I may reap bountifully. I offer to You the first fruits of my labor, being faithful in the least of things in order that I will be made faithful in much. I confess Your promise that my giving will be accepted by You as the opportunity to prepare for an abundant return into my life.

Father, my giving will be in Your proper order. I worship You as the only true God and will love my neighbors as much as I love myself. I will not tire of giving, but will remain steadfast believing, as a joint-heir with Jesus, for the harvest to come. Thank You for the provision of all my needs according to Your glory in Jesus Christ.

Now celebrate and put into action God's principles for powerful increase!

Prayer for 30, 60, Hundredfold Return

Father, in the name of Jesus, I confess the Word over my giving and financial harvest. I recognize that Your Word has established principles for giving and financial blessing and I submit myself to those principles now. As I plant my gift into Your Kingdom, I do so expecting by faith a return. I give bountifully knowing that You will multiply my gift back to me bountifully.

Lord, I also plant this seed into good ground and make plans for continued giving as I await Your miracle return, trusting in the knowledge that You give the return. I praise You now for the replanting of the harvest once it has come in. I am thankful to You for allowing me to sow back into Your Kingdom a substantial portion of the financial return. You have prepared a way for me to support Your ministry unto the earth, and I rejoice in the part I can play.

I sow my seed with a cheerful heart and without holding back from You, believing in Your Word's promise that in the manner I give out, it will be given back to me. Thank You for the faith to move mountains, and I pray, knowing and believing that the financial harvest will come as a result of Your promises. Hallelujah!

Part III
Debt: Its Responsibility, Its Reduction

5
Debt

Up to Our Eyeballs In Debt!

...the borrower is servant to the lender.

Proverbs 22:7

The amount of money the average family owes to banks, department stores, and other lending institutions has risen every year for the past thirty years. Consumer debt has increased at an even higher rate than the cost of living. It now represents a much larger *percentage* of the average worker's earnings.

Thirty years ago, only about ten % of individual earnings was being spent on consumer debt. Today, that figure has risen to a staggering nineteen %. That means almost one-fifth of the average person's earnings is now spent to service his ever-increasing debt!

American consumer debt grew by almost $50 billion in the twelve months of 1988. This brought the total to about $700 billion dollars! This means that if the present debt were to be evenly divided among every man, woman, and child in the United States, they would each owe about $2,800. Now, mind you, that is only consumer debt. This figure does not include the more than $1 trillion (1000 billion) that the American public owes to various lending institutions on their home mortgages.

The Wild Card

Today, plastic credit cards make consumer borrowing easier than ever before. These cards are rapidly adding to the whopping debt that is now taking nineteen % of all household income.

Credit cards are much easier to abuse than bank loans. The reason for this is that they do not require the borrower to fill out lengthy forms. Neither do they require him to personally sit down with a loan officer and discuss his ability to repay. Instead, many pre-approved credit cards now arrive through the mail. No consultation with the bank is necessary, so the already over-extended borrower can go out that very day and add $500 to $2500 to his debt.

Large-scale distribution of pre-approved credit cards is unique to our generation. Before their advent, American Christians were not nearly as pre-disposed to purchasing consumer goods on credit. Easy access to these plastic charge cards has resulted in the Christian community finding itself in a position of higher debt than ever before. This one strategy of the devil has done more to enslave God's children than any other.

Credit-Card Junkies

Many people in our generation are actually *addicted to credit spending*. These people have been given their own special name. They are called *"credit-card junkies."* Just like the "junk-food junkies" who cannot control their appetite for unhealthy foods, these financial junkies cannot control their appetite for *compulsive buying*.

This compulsion quickly finds them over their heads in debt. These impulsive spenders do not give a moment's consideration to how their actions will effect their already limited finances. With the mere presentation of their "plastic power," they can plunge themselves and the ones they love yet further into the "bottomless pit of debt."

One recent news story told of a man who owed the unbelievable amount of $67,000 on his multiple credit cards. With this balance, his minimum payment was over $6,200 per month. This amount represented **twice** his entire family's monthly income.

Pre-approved credit cards in the hands of a compulsive shopper can spell the end of that person's happiness. It can cause him to lose *everything he has.*

Plastic Status Symbol

The credit card has become *a status symbol of adulthood.* We all probably know a young person, just fresh out of high school, who proudly displays his first credit card. He now has plastic power to add to his status. Everyone is immediately impressed, especially his admiring parents. This seems so mature, until the card is charged to its limit in the first month.

Tiny Tot Credit Cards

A bank in Denver, Colorado, recently announced a plan to issue credit cards to children as young as *twelve years old!* It is hard to believe a society can be this irresponsible and continue to exist. Surely the writer of Proverbs was correct when he said:

Train up a child in the way he should go: and when he is old, he will not depart from it.

> **The rich ruleth over the poor, and *the borrower is servant to the lender.***
>
> **Proverbs 22:6,7**

What more can be said? Credit cards are one of the primary contributors to the debt problems of the American family. If it were only the problem of the non-Christian, it would be terrifying enough. But this same mania is rampant in the Church. Plastic power has quickly driven the average Christian to his knees, not in prayer, but under the load of debt he must now bear.

Skyrocketing Bankruptcies

Naturally, with our nation's steadily increasing credit-card debt, there comes a steadily decreasing ability to pay that debt. Daily television commercials encourage those with financial difficulty to come on down to the attorney's conveniently located offices, and he will make your money problems just go away. All of this will be done by the world's miracle of debt cancellation — *bankruptcy!*

Since 1984, there has been a sharp increase in personal bankruptcies across our nation. This number reached an alarming 550,000 cases in 1988. It is up ninety % since 1984! That's a ninety % increase in just six years!

The ease of getting into debt with credit cards, and the willingness of consumers to use them, are the major contributors to this skyrocketing increase. Add the recent liberalization of the federal government's bankruptcy laws, and the removal of the *social stigma* of bankruptcy itself, and you have an *explosive situation.*

The Counterfeit Miracle

Have you noticed there is always a counterfeit to God's miracle? Instant debt cancellation through bankruptcy is no exception. It is an attempt by the devil to counterfeit God's miraculous cancellation of debt; *but do not be deceived.* The world's ways are not God's way.

As is the *earthy*, such are they also that are *earthy*: and as is the *heavenly*, such are they also that are *heavenly*.

I Corinthians 15:48

Please note, I am not against the bankruptcy laws of our land. They are not wrong when they are applied for their *intended purposes.* There are circumstances in which they are very good. However, they are *immoral* when they become an *easy fix* for irresponsible, reckless spending.

The Banks Own Our Nation's Homes!

The one material thing that Americans have traditionally treasured throughout the decades is *individual home ownership.* But now, the very homes that provide the foundation of the American dream, and in most cases, the primary source of financial security, are being placed in *great jeopardy.*

The American tradition has always been for a young couple to purchase a home so that in their senior years, the home is debt free. This has operated as a form of security for them in their retirement years. But *not anymore.* Instead, when the mortgage is paid down, the banks are now openly encouraging home owners to borrow against their equity. Here is the shocking truth to this deception. *Thirty % of all home equity loans are used to repay other debts!*

The federal government has actually helped encourage this type of borrowing, for home mortgage interest is one of the few tax deductions remaining for the average American.

Now the purchase of new cars or other "high-ticket" items is being called a tax-smart move when bought through second and third mortgages on the home. This is being recommended by financial planners and many tax experts, because the interest can still be deducted. As a result, home equity (retirement security) has little opportunity to build. The participant remains deep in debt for the entire span of his life. He never builds the much needed retirement nest egg that the debt-free home affords!

Your Hidden Debt

Most people would be shocked if they understood just how great a hold the spirit of debt has on our nation. The average American had to work 124 days in 1989 — a whopping thirty-four % of the year — just to pay his federal, state, and local taxes!

Talk about being in bondage to the creditor! You have to work *four full months* of every year just to pay your taxes! (Please keep in mind that this does not include even one of your personal debts.)

In 1989, "Tax Freedom Day," the day the average American finally paid off his debt, was May 4. Each year this date is pushed a few days farther into the year. Looking at it on a daily basis, the average worker toiled two hours and forty-three minutes out of every eight-hour day to satisfy his 1989 tax debt! This means that every day, you had to work two hours and forty-three minutes for the government before you began to earn any money for yourself.

In 1981, the American worker paid Social Security taxes at the rate of 6.65% of the first $29,700 earned, or a total maximum tax of $1,975. In 1989, the Social Security tax rate rose to 7.51% of the first $48,000, which equals an unbelievable maximum tax payment of $3,605. Social Security taxes alone have gone up over eighty-two% in the past eight years! That is more than a ten% increase per year!

Your Total Debt Increases Daily

The federal government will collect roughly $1.07 trillion in revenue in 1990. That's up $86 billion from 1989. Surely this is enough! But, no! The Congressional Budget Office still predicts there will be a $155 billion deficit!

In March of 1989 alone, the nation's budget deficit climbed to a staggering $35.78 billion. That's up 22.2% from the same month just a year earlier!

Although federal revenues were increased 3.9%, government spending shot up 9.5%. President Bush's administration estimated the 1989 deficit would total $163.3 billion. That is an increase of 5.3% from the $155.1 billion shortfall posted in fiscal 1988.

Here's a number that should stagger your imagination: **$2,775,874,961,565.00**

That figure was calculated on April 17, 1989, by the Bureau of Public Debt. It represents the total indebtedness of the government of the United States of America on that day. That is how much money we, the American public, owed, and the amount has steadily grown since then.

On average, the national debt grows at the rate of $722 million per day! This means that by August 17, 1989, the government's debt went up approximately another $87 billion! And it shows no sign of stopping. It just keeps getting worse!

You Pay for the Banker's Party

On August 9, 1989, President Bush signed into law the biggest taxpayer bailout in history! The cost for the bailout of the savings and loan industry is staggering. Estimates are that it will total over $1,000 for every man, woman and child in the United States before it is complete. The estimated cost is $306 billion. That is bigger than the bailouts of Chrysler Corporation, Lockheed, New York City, and postwar Europe's Marshall Plan combined.

To show you just how blind a nation can become, just hear what else took place. In the same month, Congress easily passed a foreign aid package to send $14.3 billion to other nations, including $3 billion for Israel, $2.1 billion for Egypt, and $85 million in military aid to the newly elected government of El Salvador.

Also in that same month, President Bush announced the cancellation of the debt of sub-Saharan African countries to the United States, an amount that is said to be $4.3 billion!

By now, your head is probably dizzy from all these huge numbers, so let me bring it all down to statistics that will make some sense to you. If you had all of your own personal debts paid off, and if you did not owe anybody anything, your personal share of our federal government's debt would still be *$11,209.54.* Remember, this is the amount each man, woman, boy and girl owes. If you are the average American family, you have a spouse and two children. That means your total family debt is $44,838.16! (If you have more than two children, add $11,209.54 for each additional child.)

This debt increases about $3 each day for every man, woman and child. In one year, that amounts to $1,095. This dollar amount represents what the federal government has spent, above the amount they have collected. This is over and above the taxes you have already worked until May 4th to pay!

The World Is Drunk On Debt!

The spirit of debt is not limited to America. Mexico, for example, is currently suffocating under an unmanageable debt load. In 1970, Mexico's foreign debt was less than $5 billion. In just nineteen years, it grew to $100 billion.

In 1989, Mexico had to pay $7 billion in principal payments and an unbelievable $12 billion in interest to its multitude of creditors. Mexico's $19 billion *debt payment* for 1989 was almost four times the amount of their *total debt* in 1970! President Carlos Salinas de Gortari states, "The foreign debt burden has put the brakes on our national progress. It threatens to break up the entire social and economic fiber of the Mexican community. If this excessive transfer of our resources abroad persists, all will be lost."

Third-world developing countries now owe a total debt of $1.3 trillion. In 1987, sub-Saharan Africa alone owed $137.8 billion in medium and long-range debt. The amount of the payment to service these debts rose from $5.6 billion in 1979 to $21 billion in 1989. That is a 400% increase in ten years, or forty% per year.

The spirit of debt is rapidly spreading across the earth. It is more infectious than any other disease on the planet. During the eighties, Americans, like their government and the governments of other countries, have overdosed on deficit spending and debt. This has brought us to the nineties with nothing more than *promissory notes in the world's coffers.*

Going Under In Good Times

Credit counseling services report a shocking sixty-seven% increase in the number of clients coming in for help over the past four years. This rapid increase of people owing more money than they can repay would be somewhat understandable if our economy were in a state of depression. But it is not! This increase of financial problems is taking place in the midst of unprecedented financial growth in the American economy!

A Federal Reserve Board economist in Washington, D.C., says historical patterns have gone crazy. It seems contrary to logic that so many Americans would owe so much in a time when financial growth across the nation is rampant.

Tipping Instead of Tithing

The April, 1988, issue of ''Christian Retailing'' carried an article by Ralph Rath which revealed that the average charismatic Christian spends only $2.17 per week on all Christian-related items. Mind you, that's not just in tithes and offerings. It represents what he spends on *all* Christian causes!

Let this sink in! American Christians spend thirty-four% of their wages to pay Caesar (the government), while they spend less than two% on all Christian endeavors combined. This leaves God with nothing more than a tip!

A Prophetic Word

Starting right now, the word from God to His Church is, *"Get out of debt!"* The nineties will be perilous years for planet Earth. The creditor is at the world's door, and *the mortgage is due.* There is nowhere to hide. Pastors used to preach about payday someday. Well, that day has come, and the *cupboard is bare.*

The spirit of debt has driven the world into a most uncomfortable position. *Individuals,* as well as *nations,* find themselves up to their eyeballs in debt. They do not seem to realize that the end of the good life is soon to come, even though every day it becomes more obvious that ever-increasing debt cannot continue.

Worst of all, Christians have blindly followed the lost into this pit. Oh, that they might wake up before *the trap closes behind them!*

Is anything too hard for the Lord?. . . .

Genesis 18:14

A strong sense of hopelessness. . . That is the way many Christians describe their inner feelings about their finances. They feel as if they are aimlessly adrift in an endless stream of borrowing. Unpaid bills occupy more and more of their thoughts. They honestly believe there is no way out of their debt dilemma.

Please note that I am not speaking of dishonest people, but hard-working, honest folks who are doing all they know to do. However, try as they may, they keep sliding further and further into debt.

All statistics were compiled by Christian Services Network, El Cajon, California.

The Joy Is Gone

In most homes, both husband and wife are forced to work. Yet, even with two wage-earners, money always seems to be in scarce supply.

For most families, the joy is gone from payday. All that remains is the Friday night ritual of rushing the paycheck to the bank so the checks they wrote Thursday will not bounce. After the paycheck is deposited, they draw out a few dollars from the automatic teller machine for their once-a-week, Friday-night splurge. This consists of a modest meal at a fast-food restaurant and a short walk through the mall. Long gone are the days of shopping, for *they must now pay for their past credit sprees.*

For a pitiful, few hours, the wage-earner feels good, enjoying a small portion of the fruit of his labor. All too soon Saturday morning arrives, and with it comes the full reality of the fruit of debt. The wage-earner must now face his *mountain of bills* — bills that were only partially paid last payday.

God Is Left Holding the Bag

Check after check is written until, finally, the last pressing obligation is paid. With this task accomplished, the stark reality comes to light. There is only enough left to barely scrape by until next payday.

In the crushing pressure of having only enough to make ends meet, *the tithe,* which is so vital to receiving God's blessings in life, is usually ignored. At best only a portion of it is paid. This is usually justified with a promise that soon things will be better, and then God will get what is His.

For the next six days, the average wage-earner has to put off having any fun or doing anything special. To the Christian, the most painful part of his existence is *having to say "No" to God concerning giving into His Kingdom. This is an empty cycle that is routinely made from Friday to Friday by those who have come under the control of the spirit of debt.*

Wake Up to a Better Way!

Wake up! That's no way for the children of God to live! Surely this is not God's best for your life! He must have a better plan.

A Progressive Walk

God is as concerned about your financial success as He is about every other part of your life.

When you first started to walk with Him, you had to learn to recognize the lies of the devil. They were holding you captive. The world had taught you that drinking and parties were the fun way to live. But as you progressed in your Christian walk, you realized that kind of thinking is flawed. You began to understand that drinking almost always leads to alcoholism, and wild parties open the door to sexual sins. You found that if you were to experience God's best, you would have to say *"No"* to sin, and *"Yes"* to God's way of doing things.

The further you walked in God's ways, the less complicated your world became. Inner peace began to grow. Much to your own surprise, you started having more fun instead of less fun. Since the troubles and torments that accompany the world's wicked ways have begun to melt away, your life has become much more worthwhile.

Well, Child of God, I've got good news for you. This same freedom that you are experiencing in this area of your life is also available to you with regard to debt!

Recognize the Cause of Your Problem

Before you can participate in this miracle transition, it is important that you recognize some things. *Lies and deceptions* are responsible for your paycheck-to-paycheck existence. Following the world's system of finance instead of God's way is what has brought you to financial shambles. Make no mistake about it. *The world system has enslaved you.*

You must identify the subtle deceptions of this system. You must see how these lies have drawn you into your current financial problems.

The Die Is Cast In Early Childhood

Most Americans bring up their children in homes with *thirty-year mortgages*. They deliver those same precious children to neighborhood schools in the latest, most up-to-date automobiles with *five-year loans*. They buy these children new school clothes with plastic credit cards that charge as high as *twenty-one % interest* per year! They wash those same clothes in washing machines that have been financed on the department store's *revolving charge account*.

Their children sleep on *mortgaged beds*. They sit on *mortgaged furniture*. They watch a large-screen, color *television set* which will hopefully be paid off before it falters and breaks down. *Vacations* are routinely paid for with convenient *monthly payments*. The children do their homework using *encyclopedias and computers* that are bought on *credit*.

The average Christian child is *born into a family that is in debt*. During his childhood, he *never sees that family come out of debt*. Is it any wonder that after eighteen years of development under this influence, the spirit of debt has been transferred to this impressionable child?

The Ritual of Maturity

Debt has become a ritual of maturity in America. Upon graduation from high school, parents proudly take their child down to the local bank. There they lovingly co-sign a loan for his very first car. With this action, they unwittingly launch him into his own *ocean of red ink*. Parents do this, sincerely believing they have given their child a real ''head start'' by establishing his credit rating early!

That's crazy! How much of a head start is this innocent child really receiving? He will probably begin his adulthood earning little more than minimum wage, yet he will owe the bank between five and fifteen thousand dollars on, of all things, a rapidly depreciating automobile!

This new debt has not helped him out one bit. Instead, his parents have just given their permission for the bank to hold their precious child in bondage. They have helped him pledge 1,000 to 3,000 hours of his life to serve the lender!

If what I am saying sounds too harsh, just think about it for a few minutes. Remember, any truth that goes against common beliefs is never accepted easily. But please keep your spirit open, and *consider the entire matter before you react*. I am teaching a *tradition-breaking truth!*

This young adult is now deeply indebted to the bank. He has promised to pay them a whopping *twenty-five to seventy-five weeks of his pay*. This represents six months or more of his meager wages. It is an obligation that can take as much as five years of his life to fulfill. If that's not a form a bondage, *what is it?*

A Basic Premise Is Ignored

Now, what makes this premature initiation into debt even more amazing is that it is done without understanding that a basic scriptural premise is being ignored. When we bring up our children in this kind of a debt-laden atmosphere, we overlook one of *God's clear warnings*.

Train up a child in the way he should go: and when he is old, he will not depart from it.

Proverbs 22:6

But wait, there's more. There is a startling truth that the Church must learn. Scripture taken out of its biblical context usually does not clearly convey the message of God. Instead it conveys the meager thoughts of man. In our everyday interpretation of this verse, the importance of early training is said to be the main lesson. However, if you want some real revelation, look at this often-quoted Scripture in its full context.

Train up a child in the way he should go: and when he is old, he will not depart from it.

The rich ruleth over the poor, and the borrower is servant to the lender.

Proverbs 22:6,7

Amazing! Train a child to function in debt, and that child will not depart from it when he becomes an adult! How in the debt-ridden world have we overlooked this most obvious scriptural warning? Let that sink into your spirit for a moment; then read verse seven again.

The rich ruleth over the poor, and the borrower is servant to the lender.
Proverbs 22:7

Do you see what we have been missing? Train up your child to be a debtor, and you have sentenced that child to *a lifetime of servitude to the lender!*

When you consider the clear teaching of these two dynamic verses in their biblical context, you have but one rational choice. *A drastic change* must take place in your thinking and in the thinking of your children. Otherwise, generation after generation will continue to march their unsuspecting children down this deceptive road *into the eager clutches of the spirit of debt.*

A Miracle Is Needed

When I speak of a drastic change, I mean nothing short of a *miracle — a miracle that will rapidly take you out of debt.*

Does such a miracle exist? Can we actually go forward in some financial healing line and walk away with all of our bills marked *paid in full?*

"Why Brother John, if that were so, the person who had that power should immediately bring this miracle to every family in the world. And that's not all he should do! He should then go to every Church that is under the bondage of debt, and set them free."

If this type of logic has a familiar ring, it should! It is the same reasoning used by those who are skeptical of miracle healing. Those same sincere folks say, "If anyone really had the power to heal people, he should go to every hospital and heal everyone.''

If there was a man alive today who could miraculously heal people, he would be insensitive if he did not at least heal all the sick folks he met. In the same way, if there was a person who could miraculously release people from the awful burden of their debts, that person would be mean indeed if he did not do so.

Before we go any further, let us get one thing straight. No man has the ability to miraculously heal anyone! *Neither is there anyone who can miraculously release people from their debts!* Beloved, the fallacy of this thinking is that miracles are from *men*. They are not from men. Miracles are given by *God* and received, through faith, by men.

I have laid hands on many people and seen them healed; however, *I have never healed anyone.* Each time someone has been miraculously healed, that person had to receive the miracle from God.

The same biblical principle applies to *the miraculous release from debt.* Each time the miracle of debt cancellation takes place, it comes directly from God to those who receive it through faith.

A Widow Received This Miracle

Make no mistake about it. The miracle of canceled debt is taught in God's Word. One very powerful illustration involves a widow woman and her two sons.

This widow was left with a great debt at her husband's death. She was hopelessly bound until the miracle of debt cancellation set her free. Her debt was so large that her two sons were sentenced to become bond-servants to the creditor.

It took everything she had. She was left with nothing more than a small pot of oil. She was brought to the very door of destitution. In her advanced years, she was cruelly sentenced to the life of a beggar.

Thank God for her faith. Her decision not to seek help from the creditor proved to be the wisest move of her life. In the midst of her desperate problem, *she turned to her man of God.* All the creditor could offer her was *more debt,* but God presented her with the opportunity to receive the miracle of canceled debt. All she had to do was exercise the faith to do exactly what her man of God told her to do.

The following verses tell us about her powerful miracle of debt cancellation.

> **"Now there cried a certain woman...unto Elisha, saying, Thy servant my husband is dead...and *the creditor is come* to take unto him my two sons to be bondmen.**
>
> **And Elisha said unto her...what hast thou in the house? And she said,...a pot of oil.**
>
> **Then he said, Go, borrow thee vessels...**
>
> **And when thou art come in, thou shalt...pour out into all those vessels, and thou shalt *set aside that which is full*...**
>
> **And it came to pass, when the vessels were full...the oil stayed.**
>
> **Then she came and told the man of God. And he said, *Go, sell the oil, and pay thy debt....*"**
>
> **II Kings 4:1-7**

There it is, right from the pages of your own Bible! A miraculous cancellation of debt! The scriptural account of this particular event opened with an impossible mountain of debt. It demanded payment. Even if it meant the ruination of the woman and her two sons, it had to be paid. Then, in just a few hours, this woman was completely debt free!

With this miracle from God's Word, we see proof positive that He has a miraculous solution for the debt problems of people just like you and me. As you continue to read, you will learn just how badly this miracle is needed!

Debt — A Very Heavy Responsibility!

"...Alas, master! for it was borrowed."
II Kings 6:5

The story I'm about to relate to you is true. It comes from the Bible. It is so simple in its truth that most miss its intended meaning. *Debt brings a staggering burden of responsibility upon the borrower.*

We saw how debt can force senior citizens to sell their homes and move to remote locations without family and friends. We saw how individuals, and even entire countries, suffocate under the burden of debt. Let us now focus on the staggering consequence of debt as it is shown in the Word of God.

The Prophet's Attention Is Captured

The sons of the prophets were in the process of cutting wood for a new dwelling. To obtain the best beams, they went down to the water's edge where the trees grew tall and straight. As one of them was cutting down a tree, the ax head came loose and fell into the water, promptly sinking to the muddy bottom.

At that very moment, the man of God walked by. The young prophet knew he had but a brief moment to draw the prophet's attention to his desperate problem.

You may wonder why the loss of such a simple thing as an ax head would be called a desperate problem. It seems all that was needed was a voucher for the young man to be reimbursed. With the money, he could buy a new ax head, and all would be well.

Before the true depth of this young man's problem can be understood, there is something you must take into account. The Scripture says this was a very special ax head, for it was borrowed. When an ax head is borrowed, nothing but the safe return of the same ax head, in the same or better condition is acceptable.

Fortunately, this young man understood Elisha's heart. He knew the man of God did not want his people to be in debt to anyone. Because of his insight, he did not simply call out, "Sir, I've lost my ax head." Nor did he say that a very good ax head had fallen into the water. He did not cry out to the prophet that the ax head had great sentimental value, or that it had been in the family for years. Any one of these pleas would probably have brought forth no more than a word of sympathy.

Instead, this young fellow guaranteed the involvement of the man of God in retrieving the ax head by crying out that it was *borrowed!*

> **. . . and he cried, and said, Alas, master! for it was borrowed.**
>
> **II Kings 6:5**

Most people do not understand that when they take responsibility for something that is not their own, their entire emotional being will be shaken if it cannot be returned. When the young man realized he could not repay that which he had borrowed, his responsibility for the ax head immediately began to weigh heavily upon him.

Because It Was Borrowed

How did the man of God respond when he heard that the ax head at the bottom of the river had been borrowed? He immediately realized that this matter went far beyond the mere loss of an ax head. Something had to be done. Everything else had to wait, for the young prophet had allowed himself to become the servant of man (the lender).

> **. . . the borrower is servant to the lender.**
>
> **Proverbs 22:7**

Nothing short of a miracle could have solved this problem. The young prophet's moment of reckoning was fast approaching. The ax head would soon have to be returned. If it could not be, the testimony of that young man would be tarnished in the eyes of the lender.

Hear the sacred Word as it reveals the prophet's attitude toward the young man's problem.

> **And the man of God said, Where fell it? And he shewed him the place. And he cut down a stick, and cast it in thither; and the iron did swim.**
>
> **Therefore said he, Take it up to thee. And he put out his hand, and took it.**
>
> **II Kings 6:6,7**

One of the most extraordinary miracles ever performed took place. There was no other reason great enough to merit a *swimming ax head* than the fact that it was borrowed. This immediately changed the importance of this occasion from a *minor* event to a *major* event.

Often this passage is used to illustrate the power of God. Why, He can even make an iron ax head swim! But beloved, that is not the main point being made here. The most important lesson is that *God is concerned about your debt problems!*

Debt Brings Anxiety

Experts tell us that today, as never before, our society is overwhelmed with anxiety. The greatest single reason for this emotional upheaval is attributable to *money problems.* The staggering debt with which most people are forced to live is more than their emotional systems were created to bear.

Please note that I am not speaking of "financial deadbeats" (those who borrow with no intention of repaying). I am speaking of good, honest people who have foolishly acquired more debt than they can repay. Our society is full of these folks. They suffer tremendous psychological pain. Their inability to manage their debts gives them a feeling of hopelessness.

More sleepless nights are attributed to unmanageable debt than to anything else. This has been greatly responsible for America becoming an around-the-clock society. Stores, television stations, and bars remain open twenty-four hours a day, primarily catering to the needs of the sleepless.

A Damaged Fender Can Damage Your Soul

Let me illustrate how devastating the responsibility of debt can be. Have you ever had a little fender-bender with your automobile? When this happens it is traumatic, to say the least. No matter how unpleasant it may be, it is not to be compared to the trauma that the same fender-bender would cause if the circumstances were just a little different. Imagine that you had this same accident in a *borrowed car.* Upon impact, your inner man (soul) would immediately cry out, *"Alas, it was borrowed!"*

No matter how you try, it is next to impossible to completely remedy the damage that is done to something borrowed. It will never be the same again. You can even go out and buy a more expensive model to replace it, but from deep down in your soul, "the accuser" will tell you of your *irresponsibility*. Even if the lender totally forgives you, your soul may be permanently scarred. The impact of not being able to return that which you borrowed in its original condition will leave its mark. Each time you see the one who loaned you the car, you will feel the pain. Personally, I would rather have my own automobile totally destroyed than to put even a scratch on a borrowed car!

When responsible people borrow, their emotions are always impacted. There is no better way to put it. *Borrowing grinds at your insides.*

Debt Attributes to Divorce

Many Christians have a hard time believing that God is concerned about their finances. Yet all Christians would agree that God has extreme concern for the sanctity of marriage. Well, beloved, here's a simple fact. Unmanageable debt is the leading cause of broken marriages! In 1988 over fifty percent of the 1.3 million newly divorced couples listed *money* (or more precisely, more debt than there was money to repay) as *the main reason* for their divorces.

It's no wonder that financial trouble is the leading cause of divorce. When debt is out of control, wives become *afraid* to answer the telephone. They fear hearing the harsh voice of another bill collector demanding payment. They are *afraid* to answer the door because they may be greeted by one of the utility companies that has come to shut off their service. Every time a truck pulls up on their street, they *fear* it is the man from the finance company coming to take back the television or the family car.

With a day of *debt-induced terror* behind her, you can easily imagine the "warm" greeting this housewife is going to give her already stressed-out husband when he walks in the door. Can you imagine the inadequate feelings this husband experiences as he listens to his wife's broken-hearted description of her day? Do you see how debt tears at marriage?

Christian marriages are not exempt! Husbands become threatened, even intimidated, when they fail to provide the basic necessities for their families. This strikes at the very essence of the husband's manhood.

Breadwinners Become Bread Losers

Even though many wives work outside the home, the husband is traditionally looked upon as the family's *breadwinner*. However, if he fails to adequately provide bread for the family, at least in his own mind, he becomes the family's *bread loser*. Financial failure causes him embarrassment, making him feel unattractive, even unworthy of his wife's attention. When the husband begins to feel inadequate in providing the basic necessities for his family, that family is well on its way to destruction.

The results are predictable. The most intimate relationships in that marriage start to fall apart. All meaningful communication stops as the relentless *pressure* of unpaid bills increases. Loving care is quickly replaced by *short tempers*. Family fights start over such things as whether it is *really* necessary to take junior to the doctor. The real issue ceases to be whether the child needs medical attention, but the underlying issue is *"How in the world will be able to pay another doctor bill?"*

Divided Families

This same tragic pattern often repeats itself among other family members. When son borrows from father, or when sister borrows from brother, and fails to pay back the debt, something much more serious than the loss of money takes place. Fathers and sons stop talking. Brothers and sisters cease to visit each other. In short, borrowing from relatives often results in a permanent breach in normal family relations.

Broken Friendships

Bad debts quickly break up *lifelong friendships.* When you borrow money from a friend, then cannot pay it back, what happens? Invariably, the friendship begins to weaken, then it just dies. If the amount of the debt was high enough, lifetime friends are turned into *lifetime enemies.*

Good Employees Become Bad Employees

Alcoholism and drug abuse are often triggered by the pressures of unmanageable debt. Previously good employees are driven to poor work habits, crime, or even suicide over their debt problems. Sleepless nights and meaningless days are the result of not being able to pay the bills. Eventually, a good employee becomes a bad one. Letters of commendation turn into *warning notices,* and eventually, the dreaded *pink slip appears.*

The Great Commission
Becomes the Great Omission

The over-extended Christian can have little, if any, part in the Gospel outreach. Instead of his primary purpose being to reach the world for Christ, he must now allocate all his money to debt payments. To put it simply, *his debt now rules him.* He can no longer properly give to the cause of Christ. His new master will not let him. Debt always says, *"NO!"* to the preaching of the Gospel. For all intents and purposes, the overburdened child of God has, by his own hand, canceled his part in the "Great Commission."

When the spirit of debt rules, the biggest goal the local church has is making the monthly mortgage payment. Satisfying the lender has replaced satisfying God. When this happens, the Church is no longer the servant of God. Her own foolish actions have made her the servant of the lender.

Child of God, I hope the seriousness of this nightmare is beginning to sink into your spirit. *Debt rules! Debt ruins!*

Remember, the Word of God says,

> **. . . the borrower is servant to the lender.**
> **Proverbs 22:7**

Forced Bankruptcy Awaits

When you come into uncontrollable debt, no financial decision can be made without first consulting your new ruler, the lender. You cannot go on vacation. You cannot buy desperately needed groceries for the hungry. You cannot even give to the Gospel.

Even if the spirit of God moves you, the lender has the right to say, *"No, I must be paid first!* Until I am paid in full, you are *my* servant, not the Lord's!"

When debt rules, it can even decide that your tithe will not be paid! The courts of the land say so. There is a little-known law in the federal bankruptcy statutes that outlines a simple procedure that can be used by anyone to whom you owe money. This provision of the law allows the lender to tell you how you must spend your money.

If any of your creditors feel they are not being fairly paid out of your income, they can have the bankruptcy court intervene in your financial matters. The court can then tell you whom you can and cannot pay. This procedure is called "involuntary bankruptcy," or creditor-induced bankruptcy. When this happens, the government (Caesar), not God, rules over your finances. You will not be allowed to pay any tithe or offering until every cent is paid to the lenders!

The children of God must understand that when something has been borrowed, the fatal day of reckoning always comes. When it does, nothing short of *payment in full* will satisfy the lender. God knew precisely what He was saying when He declared:

> **. . . the borrower is servant to the lender.**
> **Proverbs 22:7**

Debt is surely an extremely severe form of servitude! It is no wonder that a loving God cares so much about people who are in debt — *people like you!* He does not want His children burdened with this heavy responsibility.

Here is a comforting statement for those of you who still cannot believe that God really cares about such basic things as the bills you owe.

> **Casting *all* your care upon him; for *he* careth for you.**
> **1 Peter 5:7**

God wants to take the excessive responsibility of the debtor off your back, ''for He careth for you!''

Jesus Had a Debt Miraculously Canceled

. . . thou shalt find a piece of money . . . .
Matthew 17:27

Jesus owed a debt? I beg your pardon! Jesus would never be in debt!

Isn't it strange that we cannot think of our Lord and Savior being in debt? Why, that is not the proper lifestyle or the Son of God! Now, hear me as I speak to your spirit. Whatever lifestyle is not proper for our Lord is not proper for His children either. Scripture is clear on this.

. . . as he is, so are we in this world.
I John 4:17

. . . we all . . . are changed into the same image from glory to glory . . . .
II Corinthians 3:18

Some Debts Are Unavoidable

Debts are incurred by everyone. Sometimes they are not the result of poor financial practices. I know Jesus conducted His business matters in a proper way. The debt He owed was one everyone will owe. It was in the form of a tax bill.

Now, I call this a *debt* because taxes are always paid in arrears. They are never paid in advance. My wife and I are debt free, so to speak, but we have a bill that never gets paid off. It is our taxes.

Let's read what the Bible says about our Lord's miracle of canceled debt.

And when they were come to Capernaum, they that received tribute money came to Peter, and said, Doth not your master pay tribute?
                                                    Matthew 17:24

The word translated "tribute" is the Greek word that literally means "the double drachma." This was the name of the coin used to pay the temple tax. Yes, Jesus and Peter were faced with a tax bill. Notice that Simon Peter immediately told the tax collector that His master most certainly did pay taxes.

He saith, Yes. . . .
                                                    Matthew 17:25

Surely Jesus paid taxes, for He fulfilled all righteousness. Later, Peter himself wrote that we, as Christians, should obey the laws of the land.

Submit yourselves to every ordinance of man for the Lord's sake: whether it be to the king, as supreme;

Or unto governors. . . .
                                                    I Peter 2:13, 14

Jesus said to give to the government that which belongs to the government.

. . . Render to Caesar the things that are Caesar's. . . .
                                                    Mark 12:17

Jesus Chose the Miraculous

As you look closely, you will see that Jesus actually stopped Simon Peter from paying the debt in the normal way. I believe Peter was on his way into the house to get the tax money from the treasurer, Judas. With this money, he was going to pay the tax bill for Jesus and himself.

> ...And when he was come into the house,
> Jesus prevented him. . . .
>
> Matthew 17:25

The verse tells us that Jesus stopped him from his planned action, for He had a better plan. This time the debt would not be paid from the treasury. There would be a miraculous cancellation of debt.

Jesus acknowledged the unfair way in which the taxes of this world were being taken.

> ...What thinkest thou, Simon? of whom do
> the kings of the earth take custom or tribute? of
> their own children, or of strangers?
>
> Matthew 17:25

Jesus asked Peter a question that dealt with how the corrupt tax system of this world operated. He asked him if he thought the king's children had to pay this tax. Simon said, "No, Lord. The strangers have to pay the tax." Jesus was showing Peter that the system controlling the world is corrupt. They tax strangers, and do not tax their own. But He quickly told Simon not to get hung up on this inequity. To keep from offending anyone and causing themselves unnecessary trouble, they would pay the tax, *but not out of the treasury.* Instead they would cancel the tax bill with a miracle.

> Notwithstanding, lest we should offend them,
> go thou to the sea, and cast an hook, and take
> up the fish that first cometh up; and when thou
> hast opened his mouth, thou shalt find a piece
> of money: that take, and give unto them for me
> and thee.
>
> Matthew 17:27

When this event is looked at as a miraculous cancellation of debt, it makes most Christians very uncomfortable. We can easily believe the miracle of the coin being found in the fish's mouth. However, we do not like the thought that this was a debt cancellation. We especially do not like to hear that this miracle is available to Christians *today*.

He Is Always the Same

We can tolerate a God who canceled debt in the Old Testament. Why, we are even able to accept that God would cancel debt in the millennium or at His Second Coming. But a debt-canceling God *for today* is more than most can believe!

Once again, I must say He is:

. . .the same yesterday, and to day, and for ever.

Hebrews 13:8

If Jesus performed the miracle of canceled debt in the past, He will perform it in the present. Peter did nothing to *earn* the payment of that debt. Jesus did nothing to *earn* His tax money either. Both Jesus and Simon Peter were recipients of the miracle of canceled debt. By a supernatural miracle, Peter pulled a coin from the mouth of a fish. That coin was of sufficient value to pay the tax bill for both of them *in full*.

Never once did Jesus say, ''Now, Peter, this is a once-in-a-lifetime miracle, so don't expect it to ever happen again.''

Trust In the Man of God Was Needed

One other major point should be considered here. It is of utmost importance to your miracle of canceled debt. Although Jesus Christ was God Himself, at this time, Peter only knew Him as a man. Before the miracle could be manifested, Peter had to be willing to *believe and obey his man of God,* Jesus.

If Peter had told Jesus, "Lord, you have got to be kidding. I'm not going to go down to the sea and make a complete fool of myself by looking for money in a fish's mouth. Why, Lord, I am a fisherman. I've looked in fishes' mouths countless times. I have lots of experience with fish, and I have never found a coin in one before!"

If Peter had not believed his man of God, the miraculous cancellation of the tax bill would never have taken place. Peter had a clear-cut choice. *Believe the man of God and prosper, or doubt the man of God and block the prosperity of God.*

> **. . . believe his prophets, so shall ye prosper.**
> **II Chronicles 20:20**

He chose to believe his man of God, and he prospered. The miracle of canceled debt was his. Don't you know Peter was glad he trusted his man of God when he saw his tax bill marked *paid in full?*

The Miracle of Canceled Debt

> **All scripture is given by inspiration of God, and is profitable. . . .**
> **II Timothy 3:16**

The Scripture is most surely profitable. It has been of benefit to men and women for as long as it has existed. Again and again the Bible has brought salvation, health and guidance. However, the benefit of the Word of God goes beyond this. It is effective for *every need and want of mankind.*

Back-Breaking Load of Debt

One of the greatest needs the Church faces today is release from its back-breaking load of debt. By the Church, I mean the individual members as well as the corporate structure. Debt is rampant in our midst.

Getting You Through, Not Out

The Church is hearing more prophecy than it has ever heard about the approaching end of the age. Personally, I have been hearing this message for over thirty years. I am convinced that the Second Coming of Christ is closer than it has ever been. However, it is evident that this event has not yet taken place.

This fact has caused me to begin to emphasize God's ability *to get us through* the everyday problems of life. For this reason, I have dedicated my ministry to prophesying *the solutions* God has for His people in these last days.

Please do not misquote me! I believe Jesus has the *ability* to return *at any moment.* Personally, I hope He does come soon. However, if He chooses to tarry His coming, I want the children of God to know that the answer to Satan's end-time strategy of debt is *God's miracle of debt cancellation!*

Today Is Not the Day of Miracles

Now I can just hear someone saying, "Why, Brother John, don't you know we live in New Testament times? God would never perform a miracle of debt cancellation in these days. Haven't you been told that *this is not the day of miracles?*"

I must agree. I do not believe in the day of miracles either. However, I do believe in the *God* of miracles, and there have always been people who believe *He* is able to perform miracles in *the time of their need.* Miracles do not depend upon a *day* for their manifestation. They depend upon the *ability of God,* who performs them.

However, even those who willingly accept the fact that God still performs miracles often resist the possibility that He will still perform the miracle of debt cancellation.

It Serves Them Right

Many Christians feel that those who are in hopeless debt situations *deserve* the misery they have brought upon themselves. Deliverance for irresponsibility somehow seems wrong. Why, miraculous debt cancellation would be nothing more than letting the spend-thrifts have their cake and eat it too! Those who have carefully budgeted their money just don't think it is fair for those who have purchased every *impulse* item they desire to get off *scot-free.* They, of all people, *justly deserve* the hard times their reckless spending has brought upon them. Surely they should not be let off the hook with a miracle!

The Elder Brother Spirit

This is the same spirit that overcame the elder brother of the Prodigal Son. He was not disturbed because his brother had squandered all his inheritance. He was angry because his wayward brother did not have to suffer long and hard for his indiscretions.

Please let me warn you. You must guard your heart against this kind of thinking. Remember, the deliverance of God is *always unmerited.* The spirit of jealousy that results from this kind of thinking *is no better than the spirit of debt it condemns!*

No One is Cheated When God Delivers

When a person is healed of cancer, you never hear anyone complaining, "Well, that miracle just isn't right. The doctors got cheated out of their surgical bills." You don't hear anyone saying the hospital was cheated out of their medical charges. No one says an injustice was done to the mortuary because the healing kept them from getting their fee. No one will claim that others with cancer were cheated because they were not healed.

Well, I know this thinking must sound pretty ridiculous, but I suspect these are the types of thoughts that keep most Christians from rushing to God for debt relief. Inwardly, they believe they deserve the devastation their debt has brought with it.

God Does Not Want To Give
You What You Deserve

Think of it! Every lost person deserves to go to hell. Everyone has sinned and come short of the glory of God. Many people are sick because they have abused their bodies. Those who have smoked two packs of cigarettes a day have surely earned their emphysema. The vast majority of those who are in prison deserve their sentences. However, God is daily working miracles for these same, undeserving people. I never hear anyone say, "Oh! That person deserved cancer!" or "That person deserves to go to hell!"

No one *earns* salvation. No one *earns* healing. No one *earns* God's love. All God's gifts are freely given to those who have faith to receive them. In just this way, the miracle of canceled debt is freely given. *God wants to perform it because He loves you!*

It Is Not a Religious-Sounding Miracle

We seem to eagerly accept the miracle of salvation in the lives of the grossest sinners. We openly rejoice when those who have abused their health are miraculously healed.

Then, no matter what the circumstances are that bring someone into debt's clutches, why not accept a miracle of debt cancellation?

When we see a man pictured in an evangelistic magazine with his crutches lifted up toward heaven, we say to ourselves, "Isn't Jesus wonderful? Surely this proves that God still works miracles. He is a good God, for *He is the same yesterday, today, and forever.*"

When we see the flowing tears of a small child who was once blind and can now see, we quickly say, "Isn't Jesus wonderful? He still works miracles. He is a good God, for *He is the same yesterday, today, and forever.*"

You see, healing is a miracle we can easily identify with God. But the fact that the Church does not want to hear what the Bible says about money has made God's financial miracles sound *carnal*.

Child of God, please let it settle into your spirit once and for all. Our God does *more* than open blind eyes. He does *more* than make crippled limbs straight. He does *more* than renew the rotting flesh of the leper. *He also cancels the debts of His people!*

Please add the fact that God can cancel debt to your list of miracles, for *He is the same yesterday, today, and forever! He* has saved before, *He* has healed before, and *He* has delivered from the power of debt before.

If you have a debt today, your God can perform a debt-release miracle today. Whatever He did for those in the past,

He can do for you in the present. Miracles are available *any day that a child of God has the faith to believe for them.*

More Qualified

I must point out another special truth to my readers. Today, you are actually more qualified to receive the miracle of canceled debt than anyone mentioned in Scripture. The Word of God clearly promises this.

After the writer of Hebrews carefully stated the miraculous way in which God moved in the lives of the Old Testament saints, he boldly promised that *something much better is available for us.*

God having provided some better thing for us....

Hebrews 11:40

As marvelous as any miracle in the Bible may seem to you, you have a *scriptural promise of an even better miracle!*

Now, please keep this in mind. The miracle of debt release will not happen because I say it will. It will happen because *the Holy Bible, the perfect Word of God, says it will.*

...let God be true, but every man a liar....

Romans 3:4

Your miracle of canceled debt can be better *because* you are in a *better relationship with God through a better covenant.*

Remember, miracles are not given out by man. They are always *given by God.* They are almost never given to those who doubt that they can have them. They are given to those who *receive them through unwavering faith.*

...let him ask in faith, nothing waver-ing....

James 1:6

This can be taken one step further. Just because a desired miracle does not manifest itself immediately, that does not mean it is not available. When healing does not immediately manifest itself, you do not stop believing that the miracle of healing exists.

The same is true for the miracle of debt cancellation. After you have prayed for it, just continue to do everything in your power to pay off your debt. Keep believing, and keep praying. The miracle will take place.

Through the power of faith and patience, God *can* and *does* intervene in our lives to *miraculously* heal. In that same way, through the power of faith and patience, He will also *miraculously* intervene to help you pay your debts.

> **. . . be . . . followers of them who through faith and patience inherit the promises.**
>
> **Hebrews 6:12**

No circumstance is too difficult for God. He can save; He can heal; *He* can also break *the death grip of debt* off your life!

You Have Already Manifested Your Greatest Faith

Whenever faith is mentioned, most Christians immediately think of some great, mystical task they must perform to get God moving. Let me set your mind at ease. If you are saved, *you have already manifested enough faith* to receive the greatest miracle possible — *the miracle of salvation.*

Yes, when you received your salvation by faith, you received the greatest miracle God has to offer. No miracle can ever be greater than the miracle of new life in Jesus Christ.

Now, I must point out that some strange process takes place in most Christians soon after they accept Jesus as their Savior. With the passing of time, they grow weaker in faith instead of stronger. They begin to struggle with the miracle of healing. They struggle with the miracle of restoration of family relationships. They struggle with the miracle of increase in their finances.

Unbelief and Traditions Weaken Your Faith

For a long time I was puzzled at this strange phenomenon. Then I realized that *unbelief* and *traditions* work in direct opposition to the Christian's ability to receive.

How Unbelief Begins

Please wake up to this biblical truth. *Unbelief will restrict the miracle-working power of God in your life.*

> **And he did not many mighty works there because of their unbelief.**
>
> **Matthew 13:58**

I am convinced that unbelief begins with *amazement*. When we are amazed by the miracle power of God as He moves among men, we are damaging our faith. Each time we allow amazement to manifest itself, unbelief is given an open door to enter into our spirits.

When God moves in great power, our reaction should be the exact opposite of amazement. We should actually only be amazed when He does not move. We should be amazed when a broken home we have faithfully prayed for is *not restored!* We should be amazed when the financial needs of a dedicated Christian family are *not met!*

Think about it. *Unbelief finds it roots in amazement!*

When you were a child, you were amazed by the huge airplanes your father took you to see at the airport. It seemed to you as if an impossible event had taken place when they ascended into the heavens like mighty, iron birds. But now that you are older and understand the nature of God's physical laws, the flight of an airplane *no longer leaves you in amazement.* You simply get on board, and *expect* the airplane to rise into the air because you know it can. The truth of the matter is that the whole nation actually gasps in amazement when an airplane *crashes,* not when it takes off.

Amazement comes from not understanding the nature of a thing. For instance, if you knew the professional techniques a magician used to create the illusion of sawing someone in half, your amazement at the trick would immediately cease.

Your amazement at God's movements comes from a lack of understanding of His true nature. When you fully understand God's nature, you will no longer stand amazed at His mighty miracles. You will understand that they are part of His normal activity.

Now, do not misunderstand what I have said to you. We should always remain in reverence, even in wonder, of God's sacred miracles. *But not amazement!* God can do anything the Bible says He can. Behold the wonder of His power! Thank Him for His miraculous intervention in your life! But do not be amazed, for unbelief finds its roots in amazement. It has no place in the mind of the Child of God who knows His Lord's abilities.

Is anything too hard for the Lord?...
Genesis 18:14

This verse asks a question that always brings a thunderous ''No!'' Yet, we still tend to be amazed when we hear that

God has dissolved a cancer, stopped an addiction, or changed the heart of a wayward child.

All of these miracles are easy for God to perform. Our Bible tells us He will do even *greater things* than those which are recorded in His Word.

> **Now unto him that is able to do exceeding abundantly above all that we ask or think, according to the power that worketh in us.**
>
> **Ephesians 3:20**

The power that works in us to receive miracles is not amazement, but *faith*. God can do anything!

When you fully understand God's divine nature, your *amazement will change to expectation,* for God's nature is unchanging.

> **Jesus Christ the same yesterday, and to day, and for ever.**
>
> **Hebrews 13:8**

When your amazement turns to expectation, *it has turned to faith*. Faith is what expectation is made of.

> **Now faith is the substance** [raw material] **of things hoped for** [expected], **the evidence of things not seen.**
>
> **Hebrews 11:1**

How Traditions Weaken Your Faith

How very powerful the Word of God is! It has turned the course of history many times. It has guided conquerors. It has doomed infidels. Its power is *almost* without earthly parallel. Notice I said *"almost,"* for no matter how powerful the Word of God is, there is a power on planet Earth that will render its promises invalid to you. *It is the power of any tradition you hold that is contrary to the Word of God.*

> **...Thus have ye made the commandment of God of none effect by your tradition.**
> **Matthew 15:6**

Traditions have an unfair advantage over Christians, for they come to us disguised as truth. The very people who loved us enough to bring us to Christ are usually the ones who introduce us to the traditions we receive and defend. No matter how sacred these teachings are, if they don't find their basis in the true interpretation of God's Word, *they must be forsaken.* You cannot move into God's best until you reject religion's best, your traditions.

God Is Stirring a Miracle for You

I feel a miracle beginning to stir in the spirit world for you. Your traditional lifestyle of debt, with its bondage to banks, department stores, and financial institutions, has *made a slave out of you!* This day, *the tradition of being in debt begins to crumble.* God's truth about debt is beginning to flood your spirit. You now know what debt has done to you. It has made you into a servant.

> **...the borrower is servant to the lender.**
> **Proverbs 22:7**

Oh, I have wonderful news for you! The miracle that will break the spirit of debt is on its way. In short order this miracle will bring you to the end of debt's domination. You are about to be set free. The revelation you are receiving from God's Word is leading you out of bondage.

Do not give way to fear. Breaking the power of debt in your life will not be too difficult for you to accomplish. You will be able to take hold of it *by your faith.* Now it will be possible for the Holy Spirit of God to lead you step by step into total debt relief.

Just promise yourself that you will not allow your *traditions* to make the Word of God of no effect. Promise yourself that you will not allow *unbelief* to weaken your faith. If you will help in this way, it will be much easier for God to release you into your new debt-free lifestyle.

Say the following sentence out loud right now.

"I am debt-free through the miracle power of God!"

Say it several more times. Say it until it ceases to amaze you when you hear it. By doing this, you are kicking the bad seeds of tradition and unbelief out of your spirit. You are replacing them with the good seed of God's Word.

Remember, God's miracle of canceled debt is the property of those who are able to believe Him for it.

Keep your *faith* focused on the *God of miracles,* and you will see that He can also perform the miracle of debt cancellation for you!

The Power of Debt Can Be Broken

> ...devils are subject unto us through thy name.
>
> Luke 10:17

Debt is a spirit, and all spirits *must leave* when they are commanded to do so in the *mighty name of Jesus!*

> **Behold, I give unto you power to tread on serpents and scorpions, and over *all the power of the enemy*....**
>
> Luke 10:19

> **And whatsoever ye shall ask in my name, that will I do, that the Father may be glorified in the Son.**
>
> John 14:13

First, Bind the Chief Spirit

God has given us *power* in the spirit world. However, before any problem that arises from demon spirits can be solved, *the chief spirit* must be dealt with.

> **. . . how can one enter into a strong man's house, and spoil his goods, except he *first bind the strong man?* and then he will spoil his house.**
> **Matthew 12:29**

Debt cancellation must be preceded by *putting a stop to the increase of debt.* The spirit of debt must first be bound from your finances before any significant changes can be accomplished. You will find that behavior modification becomes relatively easy when the chief spirit that caused the adverse behavior is removed.

Twelve Hundred Miles from My Bills

One night a few years ago I was in a telethon in Greensville, North Carolina. God had been showing me from Scripture that there is a spirit of debt. He showed me that not only had this spirit influenced the lost, but it had also driven *most of the Christian world* into the debt lifestyle.

When I departed for the station that night, I knew that before the audience would be able to receive the full prosperity of God, the power of the spirit of debt would have to be broken off their finances. I asked the viewers to gather up their bills and bring them before their television screens. God had told me the people should have their bills in hand when I prayed. This was the first time I ever rebuked the spirit of debt.

Just before I began to pray, my wife said we also needed this release. At that moment, our own bills were almost twelve hundred miles away. How could we partake under these circumstances?

Immediately the Holy Spirit showed me a way to take the anointing of that moment back home with me to our debts. I told my wife, "Take an offering envelope, and let's hold it up in the place of our bills."

I earnestly prayed, in the name of Jesus, that the viewers who joined their faith with ours would receive a release from the spirit of debt. Then my wife and I took that very special offering envelope home with us and placed it in the midst of our bills.

Each time one of our bills was paid off, we waved the anointed envelope in the air and proclaimed that the spirit of debt had been forever broken off our lives. We also declared openly that the miracle of canceled debt had been released to us. Then we placed the anointed envelope back among our bills, speaking only that all the bills would soon be paid in full.

We continued this process for the next few years. Then one day we burned our last bill. It was the mortgage on our parsonage! This was the first time in our thirty years of marriage that my wife and I were totally debt-free.

Steps That Will Take You Out of Debt

From my own experience, I can now say that breaking the power of debt will not be nearly as hard for you as the devil would have you believe. However, there are several definite steps that must be taken for you to succeed. Please prayerfully read the following list.

1. You must sit down with a pencil and paper and list every bill you owe. This accounting must be done before

you can launch a proper plan of attack against the havoc the spirit of debt has wrought in your personal finances.

This is not a secular approach to your problem. It is prescribed by our Lord Himself.

> **For which of you, intending to build a tower, sitteth not down first, and counteth the cost, whether he have sufficient to finish it?**
>
> **Luke 14:28**

Count the cost the spirit of debt has brought to your life. Recognize that he has been the motivating force behind your bills.

When you have the whole picture clearly outlined before you, ask God for the specific financial miracles you need to free you from the bondage of your debt. Remember to be thankful for any progress you make in debt reduction. Your first financial miracle may be *very small,* but acknowledge that it has come from God. Be sure to let principalities and powers know it is not your last financial miracle. There will be many more.

> **...faith is the substance of things hoped for....**
>
> **Hebrews 11:1**

If you are not acknowledging financial miracles, they will cease.

2. If at all possible, you should have a relationship with a good local church.

Why is this important? Because giving your tithes into the good ground is necessary to keep the windows of heaven open over your finances.

> **Bring ye all the tithes into the storehouse, that there may be meat in mine house, and prove me**

now herewith, saith the Lord of hosts, if I will
not open you the windows of heaven. . . .

Malachi 3:10

You cannot expect to reap financial miracles unless the
windows of heaven are open over your life.

3. It is also necessary to associate yourself with some
good-ground ministries such as a Christian television station,
a good Bible teacher, or an evangelist.

The reason this relationship is necessary is because you
will need a good place to give your offerings. Your offerings
will provide God with the measure He needs to pour out
your financial blessings.

4. The strong man must be bound.

. . . how can one enter into a strong man's
house, and spoil his goods, except he *first bind
the strong man?* . . .

Matthew 12:29

You must speak specifically to the strong man (the spirit
of debt). Tell him he is bound from any further influence
in your finances. To put it plainly, he must release his hold
on your money. Bind him and cast him from your life. Be
sure you do this in the mighty name of Jesus. Remember,
His name is infinitely stronger than the spirit of debt. The
Bible says:

That at the name of Jesus *every* knee should
bow, of things in heaven, and things in earth,
and things under the earth.

Philippians 2:10

You are not to be afraid when you speak to the spirit
of debt. *It is the spirit of debt who must be afraid.* You
have something going for you that is bigger and stronger
than anything the devil has going for him.

...greater is *be* that is *in you*, than *be* that is *in the world.*

I John 4:4

(I will lead you in speaking to the spirit of debt in the confession in the next step.)

5. Now lift your bills up before the Lord, and repeat this prayer. Say it out loud.

"Dear Lord,

"I know that You care for me, spirit, soul, and body. Lord, I have many bills. They are a hindrance to me. They keep me from giving to You the way I really want to.

"Lord, I believe that Brother John is a true man of God. I believe what he has taught me about the spirit of debt is true. I believe You are concerned about my bills and that You want to help me eliminate them.

"Lord, I ask You, in the name of Jesus, to break the spirit of debt from my life. I also ask you to miraculously cancel my debt.

"Lord, I believe that as this man of God and I join our faith together, something very special is being released into my life. I thank you that you have given me authority over the entire spirit world.

"Right now, I boldly speak to the chief spirit, the spirit of debt that has been sent by the devil. In the mighty name of Jesus, I declare you to be bound. I break your hold on my life and on my finances! Spirit of debt, you can no longer operate in my life! In Jesus' name, you are firmly bound, and I am loosed from your power over me!

"Father God, part the heavens for me. Let me know in my spirit that this foul spirit has been bound and defeated.

"I now speak to the East, the West, the North, the South, that the ministering angels of God come forth and begin to release the abundance of God into my life. I boldly speak that miracles must begin to take place in my finances right now. In the name of Jesus, I accept my financial breakthrough.

"Lord, I give you the glory for the financial miracles that are released into my life this day. Amen."

Say It Out Loud

Oh, Child of God, say it out loud. "The power of the spirit of debt is broken from my life this day!" Say it again and again until it rings in the devil's ears. The spirit of debt has controlled your finances for the last day.

If you are married, go immediately and tell your spouse that the spirit of debt has been broken from your lives. Join together in proclaiming your financial victory.

If you are single, tell the next person you meet that the spirit of debt has been broken off your life.

If the Son therefore shall make you free, ye shall be free indeed.

John 8:36

6
Debt-Reducing Strategies

How To Rapidly Sell A Home

Sometimes your rapid debt-reduction strategy may call for the sale of your present house so you can move to a home you can afford. In the following pages, you will find some helpful ideas for selling at a reasonable price in the shortest possible time.

Choose The Right Representative

It is usually easier for a realtor to sell your home than for you to sell it on your own. There are certain sales tools available to him which are not available to you. He has access to multiple listing services as well as other advertising methods. The dollars you spend on a *good* realtor's commission will be well worth it if he effects a fast sale at a fair price.

Your Agent Should Know Your Area

Your first priority in choosing the right company to represent you is to find an agency which has successfully sold other homes in your neighborhood. A little investigation will tell you which agents have made the most sales in your area in recent months. Remember, what you want is a "go-getter" who will work *for you.*

The more your agent knows about your particular area, the better. He should be able to tell prospective buyers about schools, churches, shopping, parks, and a number of other things in your community. The realtor *must be sold on your neighborhood* before he can sell it to someone else. He should feel that your house is a good buy for anyone who fits into your price range.

Overpriced Means Overlooked

Remember, today's buyers are looking for a good deal. Your home won't sell *if you are asking too much for it*. Let your agent help you figure out a realistic selling price. This can be done by comparing recent sales in your area. There are dependable, mathematical formulas which will tell you how much your house should sell for. If you have a reputable realtor, you can trust the sale price he suggests.

A Few Dollars Spent Will Bring Big Money

You should be prepared to spend a little money to make your house stand out. It will only cost you three or four hundred dollars to make a real difference in your home's eye appeal. How your house looks from the curb can make a real difference to the buyer.

Touch up the outside paint, especially the trim. Wash the windows, and patch up cracks in the driveway and walkways. Be sure your yard is cleaned up and freshly mowed. Rake up the leaves, and clean leaves and other debris out of the gutter. If you have hedges, be sure they are neatly trimmed. Planting a few flowers along the walkway or around trees, or putting potted flowers on the porch will enhance the outside appearance tremendously.

Cleanliness Says, "Buy Me"

Do a major cleaning on the inside of the house. Your house makes a great impression when the kitchen and bathrooms are spotless. Everything should be put away in its proper place, and if you have unnecessary furnishings, get rid of them. An uncluttered house looks cleaner and *more spacious.* Fill in any cracks in the walls with spackle and repaint. Also, be sure to remove any spots from your carpet.

Put On A Good Show

Keep the following hints in mind when you have an appointment to show your home. *If the weather is hot,* turn on the air-conditioning far enough ahead of time to cool the entire house before the prospective buyer arrives. In cool weather, the temperature inside should be comfortable, but never too hot. Put soothing music on the stereo. A fresh flower arrangement always makes a room seem special, and you can create an inviting aroma by heating cinnamon in a potpourri pot. Put your pets outdoors, and if you have a fenced yard, it is better to send small children outside, too. You don't want the buyer to be distracted or annoyed. Make the house look bright by opening drapes and blinds and by turning on the lights in every room. These few, simple things can make your house feel like home to a prospective buyer.

Be Ready To Deal

Do not let the sale be stopped by an offer to purchase your house at a lower price equal to only a few mortgage payments. Keep in mind that your next payments may be almost all interest. If you let a buyer get away and have to wait three months for another one, *you make the next three mortgage payments.* Only a few dollars of those payments will go toward the paydown of the principal.

When you decide to sell, it should be done as quickly as possible. Selling your home involves some technical aspects, so be sure you have proper professional representation.

How To Rapidly Sell A Car

In the process of selling the things you do not need, an automobile may be involved. Because of this, I am writing this section to help you get the most money possible from the sale of your car. Every extra dollar you receive will help pay off your debt.

Prepare Your Car For Sale

Before you put your car on the market, *you must prepare it for sale.* Without a doubt, a car that looks good will sell more quickly and bring a higher price. As long as there is no rust or body work needed, *it should not cost more than a hundred dollars* to get your automobile looking great.

The first step is to *thoroughly clean it from top to tire, inside and out.* A dirty car has very little eye appeal, so a prospective buyer may be turned off before he even hears about how well it runs. This in itself makes it well worth the time and expense involved in *washing and waxing.*

A Clean Motor

Especially important is a clean engine. If you cannot afford to have your engine professionally steam cleaned, you can do it yourself at the jet-spray car wash. (Just be sure to protect electrical parts by completely covering them with plastic wrap.) *A clean engine usually looks almost brand new* and is a good selling point.

A Clean Interior

You can rent a steam cleaner to clean fabric upholstery and carpet on the car's interior. There are also good cleaning solutions for leather or vinyl. Small tears can be repaired with tape or vinyl repair solution of a matching color. If your vinyl top is showing its age, purchase some vinyl renewal spray to make it look like new. Also, remember to clean out the trunk and glove compartment. Be sure you have thoroughly cleaned all dust and dirt from the dashboard.

Set A Fair Price

At this point, you will be ready to set your price. Remember that *your car will sell quicker if your asking price is fair*. To help you decide what is realistic, compare the following for a car of the same year and model as yours:

1. The price used-car dealers are asking.
2. The price private owners are asking in classified ads.
3. The blue-book value.

You should establish your price in the same range.

You Need Exposure

Once you have set the price, *exposure is the key ingredient. Advertise in classified sections* of local newspapers and other publications. Ads should be short, catchy, and should clearly list your asking price. Also *place notices on bulletin boards* at the office, supermarket, church, or any other place you can. Keep a "For Sale" sign in the window, and *make sure your car is seen.* Drive it around and park it in conspicuous places. Make sure all your friends and relatives know your car is for sale. They can help you by keeping their ears and eyes open for potential buyers. You may even want to *offer a small "finder's fee"* to the person who refers the buyer to you.

Get Your Money

Once you have made the sale, *it is best to receive cash* for your car. If the buyer offers you a check, *go with him to his bank to cash it.* Be prepared to hand him the title as soon as you receive the cash or his check is cashed by his bank.

Don't Buy A Haunting House

The purchase of a home is the largest single investment the average person will ever make. It can be a blessing, or it can be a nightmare. *Don't let this very special purchase become a bad experience.* You must be careful not to buy a home *that will come back to haunt you.*

If your home turns out to be a *"money pit,"* you will never get out of debt. If it is located in an area which causes it to lose value, your rapid debt reduction will not be nearly as rewarding.

Get These Things Right

Location: There is an old real estate salesman's saying that every home buyer should know. There are *three things that must be right* before a piece of property is worth purchasing.

1. The *location* must be *right.*

2. It is important to always buy property in the *right* location.

3. Whatever you do, when you buy, *be sure you buy in the right location.*

Every house can be categorized by its price. There are *inexpensive homes,* as well as *unbelievably expensive ones.* In each price range, you can find homes in *poor, fair, good, or excellent locations.* Even if your present budget only allows you to buy the cheapest of homes, *buy it in the best location possible.*

Try to buy in a subdivision where most houses are *more expensive* than yours. When your house is the least expensive in the subdivision, *the higher priced homes will tend to pull its value up.* Just the opposite will take place if you buy the most expensive house in a subdivision. Your house will tend to pull up the value of the cheaper homes, *while theirs will tend to pull down the value of your home.*

If you have children or are planning a family, be sure your house is located in *a good school district.* Buy a home close to parks and shopping — *but not too close.* There should be several streets of housing between you and hustle and bustle associated with such conveniences.

Choose your home in a location where the *property tax rate is not excessive.* Do not judge whether taxes are high by the rate in your previous city. Always compare taxes according to the rates in the area where your new home purchase is being made.

If at all possible, choose a subdivision with a *sanitary sewer system.* Also seek out information about what is planned for the future in your area. If such things as a *prison or a sewage treatment plant are scheduled,* pass on that area. It will not be a good purchase.

Termites: Any house worth buying is worth spending the money for *a termite inspection.* There is a three-fold reason for this.

1. It will tell you if the house has termites. If you choose to buy it anyway, as a condition of the purchase, stipulate that the seller exterminates all termites and repairs any damage they have done at *his cost, not yours.*

2. Most buyers *do have* termite inspections performed. At a later date, if you sell the house and did not have the previous termite problem taken care of by the former owner, you will have to pay for the extermination and repair for the person purchasing from you.

3. If there are termites in the home you buy, and they are not detected and eliminated, *they will eventually cost you big money.*

Electrical: The wiring in older homes is usually not adequate for today's modern appliances. There should be a complete inspection and test of all electrical switches, wiring, main power panel, and load capacity made by a licensed electrician. *Ask for a written report* with prices for repairs.

Plumbing: A certified plumber should inspect everything having to do with the plumbing and sewer. *Ask for a written report* with prices for repair.

Heating and Air-conditioning: Both the heating and cooling systems should be checked by a certified heating and air-conditioning specialist. Be sure to have the air flow to all rooms checked. *Ask for a written report* with prices for repair. Also keep in mind that heating and cooling costs can be extreme if you have excessively high ceilings.

Appliances: Ask for a guarantee on all appliances including dishwasher, garbage disposal, hot water heater, central vacuum, refrigerator, stove, and any built-ins. If any appliance is missing, for instance a stove or refrigerator, ask the seller to furnish you one at his cost. Don't be timid. The worst he can do is refuse.

You should have written warranty policies on all appliances. If written policies cannot be supplied, ask the seller to leave half the replacement cost for the appliances in an escrow account for six months. If all appliances are still operational at the end of that time, the money can then be released to the seller. If any must be repaired or replaced, the cost of replacement should come out of the escrow account.

Structural Compliance: You should ask the local building inspection department to have a building inspector meet you at the prospective house to answer questions and give you information. These are some of the questions he should answer for you. Is the home *built according to code?* Is it *properly insulated?* Are there any *zoning violations* on the house? Are there any *zoning violations in the immediate neighborhood?* Have him explain any *zoning restrictions* that pertain to the area, such as no pets, no trucks allowed on the street, other parking restrictions. You need to know everything you can about the house and neighborhood *before you buy. Have a written report made.*

Radon Gas Test: It has recently been discovered that there is a natural, radioactive gas called radon which seeps up through the ground and gets trapped inside houses. It is considered a *very dangerous gas.* There are properly certified companies which will test your prospective house for the presence of radon gas. *Ask for a written report* by a certified technician, with a price for eliminating the danger.

Garage: The most important thing about the garage is that both your automobiles fit into it comfortably. You need enough room to allow the car doors to be opened. You must also be able to get in and out of the house with packages in hand. *Actually park both cars in the garage to see if they fit properly.*

Have the garage door and the automatic opener checked by a garage-door installation company. *Ask for a written report,* with a price to correct any problems.

Exterior Finishes: Brick is preferable on all exterior walls unless it is cost-prohibitive in your area; then the most practical and commonly used exterior finish should be considered. Vinyl or aluminum is preferred on trim. Exterior finishes of these materials will save you money year after year because they do not have to be painted. If the soffits and overhangs on your prospective house are not covered with aluminum or vinyl material, ask the seller if he will have them covered for you. If he will not, ask him if he will at least pay for half the cost. If he commits to paying any portion of the job, *get it in writing.* Then deduct that cost from the selling price of the house, and *have the job done only after you have received several bids.*

Drainage: Always find out all you can about storm drainage in the prospective subdivision. Ask the seller specifically if the house you are interested in has ever had drainage problems. Also ask several of the neighbors if the area drains well. Run water on the driveway, porches, and sidewalks to be sure it immediately flows *away from the house.* It can become a nightmare if water does not correctly drain off your property. If water flows toward the house, it will be expensive, if not impossible to protect it at flood time.

Soil: Get a report from the local building inspection department as to whether the soil in your area is stable. If it contains bentonite or any other expanding soil, you must be assured that proper construction techniques were used to prevent the expansion of the soil from breaking the foundations. With this type of soil, there is also a real danger that the slab will rise or fall with the wet season. *It is better not to buy* if you cannot be assured that the soil is stable.

Earthquake Faults: These invisible fractures in the earth's surface can be a very real problem. They exist throughout the nation, *even in places where the earth doesn't shake.* Many faults creep and slip, causing tremendous damage to the homes above. Your building inspector should have knowledge of where these silent house-wrecking strata are.

Access: Check the traffic flow to and from the prospective house during rush hours. Notice if there is excessive traffic through the subdivision. Also check whether flooding ever closes roads to and from the area you are considering.

Fireplace: Always build a fire in the fireplace to see if the smoke is being properly drawn out of the house. Be sure the fireplace has a damper which operates correctly. Heating and cooling costs can be expensive if the fireplace damper does not function properly.

You should also have a reputable chimney sweep inspect for creosote buildup and loose fire tiles or brick. *Get a written report* with estimates for repairs or cleaning.

Cabinets and Closets: Be sure the cupboard space in the kitchen is ample to meet your family's requirements. You must be able to store *all* your dishes, utensils, and other kitchen items. Just because the cupboards seem to meet the needs of the seller, that does not mean they will be adequate for your needs. Take stock of each cabinet and be sure the space is sufficient. Also check the closet space. You should be able to hang your clothes without your garments hitting the back of the closet wall. You also want to be sure the house has enough extra closet or attic space for storage of your seasonal items.

Easements: Have all easements on the property *clearly identified.* Have some small pegs driven about ten feet apart on all easement lines so you can see exactly how much of your yard is dedicated to utilities. An easement could stop you from building onto your house, or could keep you from adding a pool or patio at a later date. It could also cause the inconvenience of equipment being moved across your property from time to time.

Eminent Domain: Through eminent domain, the government has the right to buy your property, *whether or not you wish to sell it.* Be sure there are no future plans for a freeway or other projects across your land. Government agencies often tend to offer less than fair market price when they take over property. Also realize that if a freeway is scheduled to come through the subdivision, or a road is to be widened, property values will usually be drastically reduced, even if your house remains, because of the noise and the undesirability of living next to heavy traffic.

Curbs and Sidewalks: If the curbs and sidewalks adjacent to the home are in poor condition, at some future time your city may decide to repair them. When they do, *you may be billed for the cost.* This is also true if your subdivision has no sidewalks. You may be required to pay the bill when they are added at a later date.

Municipal Services: Check to see that proper services are available. You need to know whether there is *garbage collection* at the curb, or if you are required to haul your own trash off to the dump. This can become very expensive and inconvenient over a long period of time. Also investigate the condition of the local roads in your area. Are they well maintained or full of potholes? If you are a commuter, you need to know about the reliability and easy access to buses or train service in the area.

Roof: Have a reputable roofing contractor or engineer check the condition of the roof. Do not rely on the realtor to do this for you. The roof is one of the most expensive things to replace. If it leaks, severe damage may be done to the structure and contents of the home. Ask the inspector to state the probable number of years the roof will last. Then carefully consider if you will be ready to replace it at that time. If not, have the seller replace it or share this upcoming expense with you. Be sure to *get a written report* of repair and replacement cost.

Swimming Pool: If the house has a swimming pool, have a certified pool repair company examine the pool and its plumbing, wiring, and motors. *Ask for a written report* of its condition and the cost of necessary repairs.

Crime Report: Check with the local police department about the crime rate in the area. Find out if there is any problem with juvenile delinquency. *These problems almost always grow worse with time.* Avoid a high crime area.

In general, take the time to check every possible thing pertaining to your prospective house. By doing this, you will help guarantee that you do not buy a *haunting house.*

Buying Insurance

No matter what type of insurance you need, there are several things you must consider before you buy. If you will carefully look at the following points, you will be more likely to purchase the coverage which best meets your needs.

Remember, *whatever you save in insurance premiums should be used to pay down your debt.*

Consult a financial advisor. He will best know your individual situation and provide you with additional advice on applying the following suggestions.

1. To the best of your ability, determine exactly *how much insurance you need.* You are throwing your money down the drain when you pay for unnecessary, extra coverage.

2. Always *shop around for the best buy.* Compare different policies and prices. Investigate what both company salespeople and independent agents have to offer.

3. Never let your agent decide what you should buy. He will be able to give you advice, but remember, *he can only offer you the coverage he sells.* That may not be what you need or want. Also, because he is paid primarily on a commission basis, he may tend to sell you more than you really need. Do not hesitate to tell one agent the price quote you received from another to see if he can give you a better deal.

4. Always *buy the highest deductible you can afford to pay.* The purpose of insurance is to protect you from serious financial loss, not to pay for things you can easily afford yourself. The higher your deductible rate, the lower your premium will be. It is smarter to agree to pay a few small expenses out of your own pocket than to pay unreasonably high premiums.

5. Never buy *a policy you don't understand.* Your policy should be written in *plain language* so you can see exactly what is covered and what is not covered.

6. Whenever possible, *make your premium payments once a year.* In most cases this will cost you less than paying semi-annually, quarterly, or monthly.

7. *Don't be afraid to investigate* a prospective insurance company. Find out if they are licensed to do business in your state. From their financial statement, determine if they are financially sound. Check with friends and other customers to see if the company *promptly pays claims.* Also check if they tend to adjust rates upward after a claim is filed. The agent should be able to give you the names of some customers you can call *for a personal recommendation.*

8. Every time you renew your policy, or at least once a year, *re-evaluate your coverage* to be sure it still meets all your needs.

Homeowner's Insurance

Most homeowner's policies insure your house, property, and personal belongings. They also give you liability coverage in the event someone suffers bodily injury or property damage on your premises. If you own your home, *you should have homeowner's insurance.*

It is generally recommended by the insurance industry that you cover your house for eighty percent of its *replacement value.* Keep in mind, this is not the same as its market value. Replacement value is the dollar amount it would cost you to *rebuild* your home at today's prices. If you allow your insurance coverage to drop below eighty percent of replacement value, the company is not obligated to pay the entire cost of replacement. *They may actually make you responsible for a percentage of the loss.*

To decide the proper amount of coverage for your personal property, you should *make a complete inventory of your belongings* to determine their dollar value. Please realize that unless otherwise stated, they are only insured for their *cash value, not their replacement value.* In other words, a piece of furniture that cost you $1,000 five years ago may only have a cash value of $20 today due to depreciation. If you want *replacement* coverage for your personal belongings, you must pay more money for it. You must also be sure your policy clearly states that *your belongings will be replaced.*

If you have valuables such as jewelry, furs, or original art, they may not be fully covered under your homeowner's policy. Talk to your agent and determine whether it is worth the extra cost to insure these items separately for their full replacement value.

Once you have determined what dollar amount of insurance you need, *begin to shop for discounts.* Some companies offer discounts for certain safety features such as fire extinguishers, smoke detectors, dead-bolt locks, and burglar alarms. Also, many companies offer a discount if your home is new or nearly new.

Tenant's Insurance

If you rent your home, it is wise to buy *tenant's insurance* to cover your personal property. If you live in a condominium or cooperative, your association fees may already be paying for insurance on a portion of your property. Find out how much coverage the association provides. Then buy only as much additional insurance as you need to make up the difference. Do not leave it to chance. Always be sure your home and personal property are fully covered.

Automobile Insurance

Automobile insurance rates vary greatly from area to area. One of the first things you can do to cut this cost is to *eliminate duplicate coverage.* If you already have a good health insurance policy, find out if your state requires you to purchase additional medical coverage on your automobile insurance. If not, your attorney or financial consultant may advise you to drop the medical portion from your policy. (Keep in mind that if you carry passengers other than those who are covered by your medical policy, you do need to be sure they are properly covered.)

If you have life insurance, there is no need for death benefits on your automobile policy. Also, if you have some form of disability insurance, you probably will not need additional disability or wage loss coverage unless your state requires it.

If you belong to a motor club, towing costs are usually covered, so there is no need to add this coverage to your automobile policy. In fact, even if these costs are not covered in some other way, consider paying them yourself if they are needed. They are generally less expensive when paid on an "as-needed basis" than paying the additional insurance premium.

When you decide how much collision coverage you need, keep in mind the insurer will only reimburse you for your car's *cash value.* This holds true even if you have insured your car for a high dollar amount. Remember, it is the value of your automobile after depreciation that will be covered, so don't buy any more coverage than the replacement cost. Another savings can be realized if you keep in mind that your collision insurance may cover you when you drive a rented car. Check your policy to be sure. If you are covered, you can waive this additional charge from the rental agency.

Shop For Discounts

Once you have determined the amount of automobile insurance you need, remember to shop for discounts. They are offered for a variety of reasons too numerous to list here.

Lock In The Rate

Always have your policy written with a twelve-month rate, even if you're paying your premium every six months. The rates on a six-month policy can be raised twice a year. Unless otherwise stated, the rates on a twelve-month plan cannot be increased during the term of the policy.

Some companies return a dividend to their customers at the end of each year when state-wide claims have remained low. This amounts to a reduction in your premium cost. Be sure you allow some of these companies to bid for your coverage.

Also, be sure to inform your agent immediately if there is any change of status which will lower your rate. For instance, if you move from the city to the country, or if you drop a young driver from your policy, your rates very possibly will be reduced.

Always check the insurance rates of a new automobile before buying it. A good sale price for a fancy sports car is not a good deal if you cannot afford to have it insured.

Life Insurance

Life insurance is designed to protect your dependents from the problems they would suffer should they lose your income.

Its purpose should be to provide a way for them to maintain their current lifestyle in your absence. The amount of protection you buy should be based primarily on what your family's needs will be in the foreseeable future.

If there are two wage earners in the family, then both should be insured. A younger couple will usually need more life insurance than senior citizens who no longer have children to support.

To decide just how much life insurance coverage you need, your first step is to calculate your family's current expenses. Now, subtract any expenses which would be eliminated by your death. Also, if your beneficiaries qualify for any social security benefits at your death, deduct this amount. Then deduct any life insurance you may already have through your employer or elsewhere.

You now have a good indicator of how much coverage you need to buy.

The least expensive life insurance is usually group coverage. Also keep in mind that it is more economical to buy one large policy than several smaller ones. For instance, a $100,000 policy is normally less expensive than two $50,000 policies.

The two primary types of life insurance are *term* and *whole life*.

Term Insurance

Term insurance is not a savings or investment plan. It is life insurance and nothing more. Compared to whole life, it is not very expensive in the early years. However, as you grow older, the premiums usually increase. At the same time, the value of the policy may decrease. Most of these policies are only good until you reach a specified age.

Since your insurance needs may decrease as you grow older, term insurance could still be the best buy for you. Most term insurance policies allow you to exchange them for whole life insurance at a later date. This is called *guaranteed insurability.*

Whole Life Insurance

As long as you faithfully pay the premium, a whole life insurance policy covers you for your entire life. This type of policy has the ability to build up a cash value as you grow older. The longer you maintain the policy, the more cash value it gains up to its maturity date. For this reason, many people maintain whole life policies as savings accounts. However, past experience indicates this is not the best way to save money.

Whole life is expensive in the early years, but the premiums do not increase. With certain types of policies, you are only required to pay the premium for a specified number of years, or until you reach a certain age. At that point, the policy is paid in full, and your coverage continues.

Your Policy Can Reduce Your Debt

If you already have a whole life policy, you might be able to use it to reduce your debt. A policy with a high cash value can be cashed out. A portion of the proceeds can be used to buy a less expensive policy, and the balance can be used to pay off some or all of your bills.

Also, many older whole life policies will allow you to borrow against them at a *very low rate of interest,* perhaps as low as five or six percent depending on when they were purchased. If that interest rate is lower than the interest you are paying on your current debts, you may want to use this method to pay your bills. But remember! *Whatever you do, don't leave your family unprotected.* If you cash in a policy, *the protection stops. It is up to you* to be sure you have adequate life insurance coverage at all times.

Health Insurance

In today's high-cost society, it is important to have a good health insurance policy. However, there are so many variables to consider in this type of coverage that it cannot be explained in this book. I advise you to shop around and discuss the many types of health insurance with several reputable agents to find the policy which best suits your needs.

How To Advertise In The Classified Section

If you have surplus items that can be sold to generate more cash, you may wish to advertise them in the classified section of your local paper. By following a few simple instructions, writing a classified ad can be very easy. Your objective is simply to tell the customer:

1. *What you are selling.* Be specific. Don't make the buyer guess.

2. *Something special about the item.* Tell the buyer why your item is better than the other advertised 25 just like it.

3. *About its condition.* Whether it is almost brand new, excellent, fair, or good, let the buyer know.

4. *The price you are asking.* Most people are shopping for a specific item in a particular price range. They appreciate knowing if your item is within their range before calling

to ask questions. *Don't waste their time or yours.* List your price.

5. *A phone number.* Let people call you to ask questions. Then if they sound really interested, give them your address. *Unless you are having a garage sale,* it is not necessary to put your address in the ad.

Your ad may look something like this:

86 Astro Van. Custom interior. New tires. Only 25,000 miles. Excellent Condition. $8000. 777-7777 days, 333-3333 after 6.

You may get some good ideas by reading a few classified ads in your local newspaper and noting the ones that ''grab'' your attention.

When you place your ad, the representative from the publication you choose will help you with details such as abbreviating common words and how to say the most for the least amount of money. *Don't be afraid to ask for help.*

How To Have A Money-Making Garage Sale

A garage sale can be a great way to help pay down your total debt. Don't be afraid. It's not too hard once you know how.

The Best Days

Generally, weekends are the best times for garage sales — Friday, Saturday, or Sunday afternoon. Two-day sales give *twice* the opportunity to make money.

Fridays seem to be the best days because the children are in school, Dad is working, and many moms are free to go treasure hunting. Some people set aside Fridays just for rummaging. Also remember that Friday is payday for most people.

Although many people have other things to do, Saturdays can still be excellent sale days. And for those who work during the week, Saturdays and Sunday afternoons are the only days available.

A few people always have sales in the middle of the week because they feel they have less competition, and everyone who is bargain hunting will be sure to come.

Long holiday weekends are usually not the best times for a sale. Many families make special plans or go out of town. Even those who are driving around during these days are usually going somewhere special. Generally, this is not conducive to a successful sale. However, if you are fortunate enough to live on the main road to the lake or local tourist attraction, you will have a "captive audience" on holidays. Many travelers won't be able to resist stopping to see your wares.

The Best Season

Unless you are fortunate enough to live where it is perpetually spring, the best times of the year seem to be late spring, late summer, or early fall. These are the times when more people are out and about. Cold temperatures or rain do not provide the best setting for a successful sale. Avoid these seasons if at all possible.

Also remember that just before school starts, many mothers are looking for quality, used school clothing.

The Best Time

Most customers can't get to your sale before 8:00 a.m. However, there are many collectors and antique shop buyers who fiercely compete to find the real treasures. They will usually show up as early as you want to open your sale. Many are up when their newspapers arrive. They read the ads and carefully select the route they can take to hit the most sales in the shortest time. If you open before full daylight, you *must* have excellent lighting on your merchandise, or your customers will soon be on their way.

Generally, most of your customers will have come and gone by mid-afternoon. But if you have nothing else you must do, it can sometimes pay to leave your sale open until around 5:00 p.m. Don't close up too early, for you may get a late customer who will purchase a lot of your "leftovers."

In some communities it is becoming common for working people to hold evening sales in the summer. These sales begin around 6:30 p.m. and continue until 9:00 p.m., or dark. This can bring in a completely different crowd. Those who work during the day, those who are out for a drive, and evening walkers often like to stop and browse.

Advertising

Proper advertising can make the difference in whether or not your sale is successful. Be sure people know what you are offering and how to find you. An advertisement in your local newspapers' "garage sales" column should be brief, but enticing. Be sure to list a few of your most interesting items, your opening time and complete address. Give easy directions if you are a bit "out of the way."

Such items as baby clothes and furnishings, antiques and collectibles, tools or furniture are often sought after and should be mentioned in your ad. Also place your ad in your neighborhood weekly tabloid. These ads are usually very inexpensive but require advance notice, so plan ahead.

A *large sign* with *"Garage Sale"* and your address should be placed at all main intersections leading to your house and also in your front yard. (Check local regulations regarding placement of signs.) Using black paint or waterproof markers, neatly print your sign in letters large enough to be easily read a half block away. If possible, have someone check periodically to be sure your signs are still in place — especially if the day is quite breezy.

Another sign should be placed in your yard indicating "Back Yard" or other directions if entrance to your sale cannot be seen from the street. It is advisable to have some part of your sale *clearly visible* if possible. People hesitate to stop if they do not see an open garage door or a yard full of sale items.

You can also attract attention with helium-filled balloons tied to your signs and strips of colorful banners in your front yard. This gives your sale an *inviting, carnival-like atmosphere*. If you are really ambitious, you can make scarecrow-type signs from two pieces of wood draped with a dress, topped with a hat, and your sale sign stapled to the "arm."

Put your signs up the night before, or in the early morning of your sale day. If you have time and your sale is large, you may wish to put up handbills on bulletin boards at your neighborhood supermarkets, laundromats, or churches. (Be sure to *courteously remove all signs* as soon as your sale ends.) Handbills delivered to the people in your neighborhood will also help stir interest.

Scout The Competition

If you are not a regular garage sale customer, it will pay to spend two or three weekends scouting such events for ideas. At least try to get up early on a Friday or Saturday morning and stop at several sales. You will learn a lot about pricing, display of goods and advertising. Tell everyone you know that you are getting ready to have your own sale, and ask for their experienced advice. Most people love to help by giving you ideas.

Trash Or Treasure — Be Sure You Know

You have heard that "one man's trash is another man's treasure." Be sure what you consider *trash* isn't actually a *treasure* before you sell it too cheaply. A visit to your local flea market should educate you. Those old, chipped enamel kitchen utensils you remember your mom using, and the ugly little Christmas ornaments Grandma had *may be worth a small fortune.* Old baseball cards, comics, Valentine cards, banks, kitchenware, glassware, quilts, vintage clothing and jewelry are often highly sought after. (In fact, if you have a lot of this type of merchandise, including some antique furniture, you might do well to hold a well-advertised *auction.* Collectors and dealers bidding against each other can sometimes raise prices unbelievably high.)

Ready To Get Ready

Now you are ready to get ready for your sale. How do you display your merchandise? *Neatness counts in a big way.* Toys should be clean and all pieces included. Clothing should be clean, ironed and plainly priced and sized. Glassware and kitchenware need to be free of grease and dust. Remember, if you wouldn't want to buy it and clean it up, others will probably feel the same way.

Be sure you have plenty of table space and have all items neatly displayed and legibly priced. Household bric-a-brac, records, books and such should be priced under a dollar. Exceptions include Elvis and other collectible "oldies" record albums and very old collectible books and cookbooks. These may bring considerably more money. Appliances and electronics will bring up to one-third retail value if in good condition. If clothing is currently in style and in excellent condition, you may get up to one-fourth retail value.

Helpful Hints

You should have about thirty dollars in cash in your "bank" at the start of your sale. Most of it should be in one-dollar bills. You should also have about five dollars in change — mostly quarters.

Keep jewelry and smaller valuable collectibles near you in order to be able to carefully watch them. Yes, unfortunately, some people do steal — even at garage sales.

You may want to bring out a pot of coffee or lemonade and cookies. This gives you something to ward off hunger during the sale.

Have plenty of paper and pens handy. If people wish to leave lower bids on certain items, you will be able to let them jot down their phone numbers. If you have a small adding machine with tape, plug it in near your cash box. It will be really handy to accurately total a long list of items. If you are selling any electrical items, have an electrical outlet or extension cord nearby so customers can test them. If you provide a private corner for trying on clothing, be sure to monitor how many garments go in and out. Some people have been known to hide clothing under their outer clothes while in the dressing room.

If your merchandise doesn't seem to be moving as fast as you would like, you can always tack up a "No reasonable offer refused" sign, or "Half Price Sale Today" banner on the second day. You may also want to haggle. If someone offers you $5 for an item marked $10, you can counter with a price of $7.50. You may want to put several miscellaneous items in a *free* box just to get rid of them. It also works wonders if you have a box of toys or trinkets to give small children something to do so their mothers can shop in peace.

Watch Your Cash

Be sure to keep a *close watch* on your cash box at all times, and carry it with you if you must go inside and no one is helping you. If you have a large sale, you really do need a *helper,* especially during the *early rush* of customers. Determine ahead of time if you are willing to accept checks. If so, be sure they are drawn on local banks and the writer has a picture I.D. The phone number should be included on the check, *especially on big-ticket items.*

Figure Your Profit

After the sale is over, don't forget to deduct your starting cash and your advertising costs from your total intake to determine your net profit. *You will probably be pleasantly surprised* at how well you did!

*   *   *

Prayer for War on Debt

Gather together all of your bills and any statements that will qualify your debt before you pray this debt-cancellation prayer.

Father, I pray and confess Your promises over my finances this day. Your Word plainly and clearly states that no problem or situation is too hard for You. Knowing that You have provided a better way for me to live than as a servant to the lender, I accept Your promise of miracle debt cancellation. As You have performed financial miracles in Your Word, I stand in agreement with the Word of God for the same miracles in my life.

Your Word declares, Father, that You are no respecter of persons, and that what You have done for others, You will also do for me. I take all authority over the spirit of debt in Jesus' name and bind the strong man from spoiling my house. My finances are free from the bondage of accumulating debt. Satan, in the name of Jesus, you are defeated!

I hold the bills and statements of debt in my hand and cast the cares and burdens of this debt onto You. Father, I am debt free through Your miracle power. As I continue to confess this miracle with my mouth, I commit now to be faithful in my giving of tithes and offerings into Your Kingdom. As stated in Malachi 3:10, when I bring my tithes into the storehouse (my church), You will open the windows of heaven and I will receive an overflowing blessing!

Father, I pray this as my confession of faith, opening the door for You to operate on my behalf. My faith in You is unwavering, giving no place to unbelief. I am confident of my miracle debt cancellation. Thank You, Lord, for the abundance of provision in my house and in my family.

Now, as you continue to be faithful in your giving, confess this out loud until it is your statement of fact — "*I am debt-free through the miracle power of God.*"

Rapid Debt Reduction

This prayer is for the success and wisdom of God to be upon the task you may undertake, whether it be buying a home or car or insurance, selling a home or car, or having a garage sale. Pray and stand in faith!

Father, in the name of Jesus, I confess Your Word that it shall not return unto You void, but it shall accomplish what it says it will do. I commit my tasks unto You, Lord, knowing that You shall supply all my need according to Your riches in glory, as a joint-heir with Your Son.

As Your child, I recognize and hear Your voice, listening not to the voice of a stranger. I am filled with the knowledge of Your will in all wisdom and spiritual understanding, being successful in every good thing I do. According to James 1:5,6, I ask for wisdom, standing unwavering in faith that You will direct my steps and grant me the understanding of Your will. As I make a decision regarding (buying/selling a home, buying insurance or buying/selling a car), I stand in the perfect will of God with the mind of Christ, knowing that the entrance of Your words brings light of Your sufficiency.

Satan, in the name of Jesus, I bind you from my (sale of my house, garage sale, etc.) and command you to be gone, knowing that whatever I bind on earth shall be bound in heaven. With that same word, I loose the ministering spirits to go and bring the buyers to the (sale of my house, garage sale, etc.), living by the faith of the Son of God, who has come that I might have life more abundantly.

Father, I thank You for favor and good understanding in Your sight and man's, that whatever I do shall prosper and be a success. Praise You for the mighty triumph in Christ!

Scriptures on Finances

Genesis 14:18-20

And Melchizedek king of Salem brought forth bread and wine: and he was the priest of the most high God.

And he blessed him, and said, Blessed be Abram of the most high God, possessor of heaven and earth:

And blessed be the most high God, which hath delivered thine enemies into thy hand. And he gave him tithes of all.

Genesis 26:12

Then Isaac sowed in that land, and received in the same year an hundredfold: and the Lord blessed him.

Deuteronomy 6:3

Hear therefore, O Israel, and observe to do it; that it may be well with thee, and that ye may increase mightily, as the Lord God of thy fathers hath promised thee, in the land that floweth with milk and honey.

Deuteronomy 8:18

But thou shalt remember the Lord thy God: for it is he that giveth thee power to get wealth, that he may establish his covenant which he sware unto thy fathers, as it is this day.

Deuteronomy 14:28

At the end of three years thou shalt bring forth all the tithe of thine increase the same year, and shalt lay it up within thy gates.

Deuteronomy 16:17

Every man shall give as he is able, according to the blessing of the Lord thy God which he hath given thee.

Deuteronomy 24:19

When thou cuttest down thine harvest in thy field, and hast forgot a sheaf in the field, thou shalt not go again to fetch it: it shall be for the stranger, for the fatherless, and for the widow: that the Lord thy God may bless thee in all the work of thine hands.

Deuteronomy 28:1,2

And it shall come to pass, if thou shalt hearken diligently unto the voice of the Lord thy God, to observe and to do all his commandments which I command thee this day, that the Lord thy God will set thee on high above all nations of the earth:

And all these blessings shall come on thee, and overtake thee, if thou shalt hearken unto the voice of the Lord thy God.

Deuteronomy 29:9

Keep therefore the words of this covenant, and do them, that ye may prosper in all that ye do.

Joshua 1:8

This book of the law shall not depart out of thy mouth; but thou shalt meditate therein day and night, that thou mayest observe to do according to all that is written therein: for then thou shalt make thy way prosperous, and then thou shalt have good success.

2 Chronicles 20:20

And they rose early in the morning, and went forth into the wilderness of Tekoa: and as they went forth, Jehoshaphat stood and said, Hear me, O Judah, and ye inhabitants of Jerusalem; Believe in the Lord your God, so shall ye be established; believe his prophets, so shall ye prosper.

Job 36:11

If they obey and serve him, they shall spend their days in prosperity, and their years in pleasures.

Job 42:12

So the Lord blessed the latter end of Job more than his beginning: for he had fourteen thousand sheep, and six thousand camels, and a thousand yoke of oxen, and a thousand she asses.

Psalm 23:1

The Lord is my shepherd; I shall not want.

Psalm 23:5,6

Thou preparest a table before me in the presence of mine enemies: thou anointest my head with oil; my cup runneth over. Surely goodness and mercy shall follow me all the days of my life: and I will dwell in the house of the Lord for ever.

Psalm 34:10

The young lions do lack, and suffer hunger: but they that seek the Lord shall not want any good thing.

Psalm 35:27

Let them shout for joy, and be glad, that favour my righteous cause: yea, let them say continually, Let the Lord be magnified, which hath pleasure in the prosperity of his servant.

Psalm 37:25

I have been young, and now am old; yet have I not seen the righteous forsaken, nor his seed begging bread.

Psalm 66:12

Thou hast caused men to ride over our heads; we went through fire and through water: but thou broughtest us out into a wealthy place.

Psalm 68:19

Blessed be the Lord, who daily loadeth us with benefits, even the God of our salvation.

Psalm 84:11

For the Lord God is a sun and shield: the Lord will give grace and glory: no good thing will he withhold from them that walk uprightly.

Psalm 112:1-3

Praise ye the Lord. Blessed is the man that feareth the Lord, that delighteth greatly in his commandments.

His seed shall be mighty upon earth: the generation of the upright shall be blessed.

Wealth and riches shall be in his house: and his righteousness endureth for ever.

Psalm 112:5

A good man sheweth favour, and lendeth: he will guide his affairs with discretion.

Psalm 112:9

He hath dispersed, he hath given to the poor; his righteousness endureth for ever; his horn shall be exalted with honour.

Psalm 126:6

He that goeth forth and weepeth, bearing precious seed, shall doubtless come again with rejoicing, bringing his sheaves with him.

Psalm 132:15

I will abundantly bless her provision: I will satisfy her poor with bread.

Proverbs 3:9,10

Honour the Lord with thy substance, and with the firstfruits of all thine increase:

So shall thy barns be filled with plenty, and thy presses shall burst out with new wine.

Proverbs 6:6-8

Go to the ant, thou sluggard; consider her ways, and be wise:

Which having no guide, overseer, or ruler,

Provideth her meat in the summer, and gathereth her food in the harvest.

Proverbs 10:22

The blessing of the Lord, it maketh rich, and he addeth no sorrow with it.

Proverbs 11:16

A gracious woman retaineth honour: and strong men retain riches.

Proverbs 11:24,25

There is that scattereth, and yet increaseth; and there is that withholdeth more than is meet, but it tendeth to poverty. The liberal soul shall be made fat: and he that watereth shall be watered also himself.

Proverbs 12:11

He that tilleth his land shall be satisfied with bread: but he that followeth vain persons is void of understanding.

Proverbs 12:24

The hand of the diligent shall bear rule: but the slothful shall be under tribute.

Proverbs 13:4

The soul of the sluggard desireth, and hath nothing: but the soul of the diligent shall be made fat.

Proverbs 13:11

Wealth gotten by vanity shall be diminished: but he that gathereth by labour shall increase.

Proverbs 13:22

A good man leaveth an inheritance to his children's children: and the wealth of the sinner is laid up for the just.

Proverbs 14:23

In all labour there is profit: but the talk of the lips tendeth only to penury.

Proverbs 15:6

In the house of the righteous is much treasure: but in the revenues of the wicked is trouble.

Proverbs 17:8

A gift is as a precious stone in the eyes of him that hath it: whithersoever it turneth, it prospereth.

Proverbs 19:14

House and riches are the inheritance of fathers: and a prudent wife is from the Lord.

Proverbs 19:17

He that hath pity upon the poor lendeth unto the Lord; and that which he hath given will he pay him again.

Proverbs 20:13

Love not sleep, lest thou come to poverty; open thine eyes, and thou shalt be satisfied with bread.

Proverbs 21:5

The thoughts of the diligent tend only to plenteousness; but of every one that is hasty only to want.

Proverbs 22:4

By humility and the fear of the Lord are riches, and honour, and life.

Proverbs 22:29

Seest thou a man diligent in his business? he shall stand before kings; he shall not stand before mean men.

Proverbs 28:19,20

He that tilleth his land shall have plenty of bread: but he that followeth after vain persons shall have poverty enough.

A faithful man shall abound with blessings: but he that maketh haste to be rich shall not be innocent.

Proverbs 28:27

He that giveth unto the poor shall not lack: but he that hideth his eyes shall have many a curse.

Ecclesiastes 5:18,19

Behold that which I have seen: it is good and comely for one to eat and to drink, and to enjoy the good of all his labour that he taketh under the sun all the days of his life, which God giveth him: for it is his portion.

Every man also to whom God hath given riches and wealth, and hath given him power to eat thereof, and to take his portion, and to rejoice in his labour; this is the gift of God.

Isaiah 1:19

If ye be willing and obedient, ye shall eat the good of the land.

Isaiah 48:15

I, even I, have spoken; yea, I have called him: I have brought him, and he shall make his way prosperous.

Isaiah 48:17

Thus saith the Lord, thy Redeemer, the Holy One of Israel; I am the Lord thy God which teacheth thee to profit, which leadeth thee by the way that thou shouldest go.

Malachi 3:10

Bring ye all the tithes into the storehouse, that there may be meat in mine house, and prove me now herewith, saith the Lord of hosts, if I will not open you the windows of heaven, and pour you out a blessing, that there shall not be room enough to receive it.

Matthew 5:42

Give to him that asketh thee, and from him that would borrow of thee turn not thou away.

Matthew 6:25-33

Therefore I say unto you, Take no thought for your life, what ye shall eat, or what ye shall drink; nor yet for your body, what ye shall put on. Is not the life more than meat, and the body than raiment?

Behold the fowls of the air: for they sow not, neither do they reap, nor gather into barns; yet your heavenly Father feedeth them. Are ye not much better than they?

Which of you by taking thought can add one cubit unto his stature?

And why take ye thought for raiment? Consider the lilies of the field, how they grow; they toil not, neither do they spin:

And yet I say unto you, That even Solomon in all his glory was not arrayed like one of these.

Wherefore, if God so clothe the grass of the field, which to day is, and to morrow is cast into the oven, shall he not much more clothe you, O ye of little faith?

Therefore take no thought, saying, What shall we eat? or, What shall we drink? or, Wherewithal shall we be clothed?

(For after all these things do the Gentiles seek:) for your heavenly Father knoweth that ye have need of all these things.

But seek ye first the kingdom of God, and his righteousness; and all these things shall be added unto you.

Mark 4:8

And other fell on good ground, and did yield fruit that sprang up and increased; and brought forth, some thirty, and some sixty, and some an hundred.

Mark 10:29,30

And Jesus answered and said, Verily I say unto you, There is no man that hath left house, or brethren, or sisters, or father, or mother, or wife, or children, or lands, for my sake, and the gospel's,

But he shall receive an hundredfold now in this time, houses, and brethren, and sisters, and mothers, and children, and lands, with persecutions; and in the world to come eternal life.

Luke 6:38

Give, and it shall be given unto you; good measure, pressed down, and shaken together, and running over, shall men give into your bosom. For with the same measure that ye mete withal it shall be measured to you again.

Luke 10:7

And in the same house remain, eating and drinking such things as they give: for the labourer is worthy of his hire. Go not from house to house.

Luke 12:31

But rather seek ye the kingdom of God; and all these things shall be added unto you.

Luke 12:34

For where your treasure is, there will your heart be also.

Romans 8:32

He that spared not his own Son, but delivered him up for us all, how shall he not with him also freely give us all things?

Romans 12:11

Not slothful in business; fervent in spirit; serving the Lord.

Romans 13:8

Owe no man any thing, but to love one another: for he that loveth another hath fulfilled the law.

1 Corinthians 16:2

Upon the first day of the week let every one of you lay by him in store, as God hath prospered him, that there be no gatherings when I come.

2 Corinthians 8:9

For ye know the grace of our Lord Jesus Christ, that, though he was rich, yet for your sakes he became poor, that ye through his poverty might be rich.

2 Corinthians 9:6,7

But this I say, He which soweth sparingly shall reap also sparingly; and he which soweth bountifully shall reap also bountifully.

Every man according as he purposeth in his heart, so let him give; not grudgingly, or of necessity: for God loveth a cheerful giver.

Galatians 6:6-9

Let him that is taught in the word communicate unto him that teacheth in all good things.

Be not deceived; God is not mocked: for whatsoever a man soweth, that shall he also reap.

For he that soweth to his flesh shall of the flesh reap corruption; but he that soweth to the Spirit shall of the Spirit reap life everlasting.

And let us not be weary in well doing: for in due season we shall reap, if we faint not.

Ephesians 3:20

Now unto him that is able to do exceeding abundantly above all that we ask or think, according to the power that worketh in us.

Philippians 4:15-17

Now ye Philippians know also, that in the beginning of the gospel, when I departed from Macedonia, no church communicated with me as concerning giving and receiving, but ye only.

For even in Thessalonica ye sent once and again unto my necessity.

Not because I desire a gift: but I desire fruit that may abound to your account.

Philippians 4:19

But my God shall supply all your need according to his riches in glory by Christ Jesus.

2 Thessalonians 3:10

For even when we were with you, this we commanded you, that if any would not work, neither should he eat.

1 Timothy 5:8

But if any provide not for his own, and specially for those of his own house, he hath denied the faith, and is worse than an infidel.

1 Timothy 6:17

Charge them that are rich in this world, that they be not highminded, nor trust in uncertain riches, but in the living God, who giveth us richly all things to enjoy.

2 Peter 1:3

According as his divine power hath given unto us all things that pertain unto life and godliness, through the knowledge of him that hath called us to glory and virtue.

3 John 2

Beloved, I wish above all things that thou mayest prosper and be in health, even as thy soul prospereth.

*   *   *

Prayer for Paying the Tithe

Today, I give back the first fruits of my labor and set them before You. I pray this day to You, Lord, that I have come into the promises which You have given me. I was a sinner cursed to die, but have entered into the land of my inheritance and possess that which you have given me. I was in bondage, struggling to live until I cried out to You, and You heard my voice and greatly delivered me out of my affliction and oppression, into the Kingdom of Your dear Son.

You have brought me into a new place, filled with abundance. I set my tithe before You, Lord, and praise You for the tithe! Thank You for all of the great things You have given my house. I say to You, Lord, I have given You all of the precious things in my house and have given unto those who have needed things, as You commanded me to. I have kept Your commandments and not forgotten them.

Having done all that has been asked of me, I pray that You will look down from Your habitation and bless me as Your Word promises. As I have brought the tithe to Your church, I ask You to prove Yourself, as You said in Malachi 3:10. I expect that the windows of heaven will open wide over my life. Father, I thank You that the devourer has been rebuked for my sake and You will not allow him to destroy my harvest.

Father, I praise You that as I give my offerings to you, You will multiply them back to me through the windows of heaven that my tithe has opened. I know it will come back to me pressed down, shaken together, and running over will You pour back into my house. I give freely and abundantly trusting in the promise of the abundant return. Thank You Father!

This prayer has been taken from Deuteronomy 26: 1-15, Malachi 3:10,11, and Luke 6:38.

Prayer for Finding a New Job or Improving Your Present One

Father, in the name of Jesus, I confess Your Word and the principles found in Your Word over my job search/present job. I pray this now trusting that You shall perform Your Word, and it will not return to You void, but will do that which it says it will do. I thank You in advance for my new job/improvements in my job. I know You are faithful to those who love and serve You!

I stand fast in my faith, desiring to owe no man anything other than love. I am strong, and I walk in honesty in all situations, performing to the best of my ability. I expect the increase so that I will not need anything but am prosperous in every area of my life. Lord, You have given me favor in the sight of all men and have increased my wisdom and my position before men as the result of my diligence to You.

I will not be afraid and compromise with any man or any situation. I have Your strength, and You will help me stand strong in honesty and integrity. My family is blessed because of my search for integrity through You. I avoid situations and men who cause trouble. Because of my salvation through Your Son, Jesus, I possess the peace of God which brings wisdom and confidence in all situations. I am able to do all things through Your Son Who strengthens me.

Father, I thank You that since You are the most High in my life, I have wisdom and direction from You. I trust in Your wisdom with all of my heart and am joyful in that wisdom; I prosper and receive promotions because of it. I am known in my new job/current job as a man/woman who has been promoted and placed in a position of authority because I am a servant of the Most High God Who has taught me how to be a good employee. I am prosperous and honored before all because of You.

In my new job/present job, I possess a drive to succeed because of Your call in my life. You have given me strength to do all things, and I make the best of every moment, wasting none of my time, but maximizing and economizing my hours. Lord, I thank You that my inspiration and creativity comes from You.

You have given me grace and favor with all men through my relationship with Your Son. I praise You for Your greatness!

Prayer for Success

This prayer is for preparation of success. It can be prayed for a business, a ministry, a church or for your life in general. God's principles are unchanging!

Heavenly Father, You have told us that when Your Word is present, light and understanding are also present. I thank You that Your Word will not return to You void but will accomplish what it says it will do. As Your child, I am a joint-heir with Jesus to the treasures of Heaven. I have been delivered into the Kingdom of Your dear Son. All areas of my life are better because of my relationship with You.

I confess Your Word over every area of my life. I want You to prosper my business/ministry/church/ _____. You have supplied for all of my need, and have ensured that abundance is in store. I dispatch the ministering spirits to go forth and bring in the customers/partners/members/provisions for each situation. As I walk in the knowledge of You, Father, You prosper me in each good work. I commit to You my business/ministry / church / _____. I am making my plans in accordance with Your Word. I believe they will be established and blessed by You. I submit my business / ministry / church / _____ to You. I will operate in a way that will be pleasing to You. I recognize that all sufficiency and prosperity comes from You. I open my spirit to receive Your blessings.

Satan, according to Matthew 18:18, I bind you from my business / ministry / church / _____ in the name of Jesus. You cannot steal, destroy or kill my business / ministry / church / _____.

Father, I praise You that Your Son has come to give life more abundantly! I thank You that You are my strength and have given my business / ministry / church / _____ success. I confess Your promises of success for my business / ministry / church / _____ as You guide my steps. I pray that as my spirit grows and prospers, my business / ministry / church / _____ will also grow. I will remain diligent at my work, not becoming weary in well doing. I rely upon You as the Source of my rewards.

As a sheep knows his shepherd's voice, I recognize and obey Your voice. I pray to be filled with Your wisdom and spiritual understanding. In areas where I have no experience or wisdom, I ask for it as Your Word commands me. I thank You in advance for the wisdom and counsel of Your Holy Spirit. You will give me understanding in all things if I will only ask You! I stand in unwavering faith, waiting for direction from You. I am diligent and committed to Your Word. My life, my health and my business / ministry / church / _____ are based upon its principles.

Thank You, Father, for success! You are great and mighty and deserving of praise!

Additional copies are available from your local bookstore, or from:
Harrison House • P.O. Box 35035 • Tulsa, OK 74153